FEARLESS FLIGHT

The Amazing Adventures of Wiley Post

ADAPTED BY
ERIC DABNEY & JANICE JOHNSON

ILLUSTRATED BY
SHERRY TIPTON-SNYDER

SERIES EDITOR
GINI MOORE CAMPBELL

Printed in the United States of America.

ISBN 9781 885596758

Library of Congress Control Number
2009921017

Designed by Kris Vculek

OKLAHOMA HERITAGE ASSOCIATION BOARD OF DIRECTORS

CONTENTS

CHARACTER IN ACTION

- To Our Readers -

In his book *Character is Destiny*, John McCain writes of individuals who demonstrated remarkable strength of character. He says, "…It is your character, and your character alone, that will make your life happy or unhappy…And you choose it. No one else can give it to you or deny it to you…Others can encourage you to make the right choices or discourage you. But you choose." [1]

The life stories he presents are of individuals who made exceptionally difficult choices as they faced some of life's toughest obstacles. He movingly recounts his experience as he was held in a Vietnamese prison where he observed men being tortured for information by their captors. They were told that if they would just make a statement no one would know. "…Just say it, and we will spare you any more pain, they promised, and no one, no one will know. But the men I had the honor of serving with always had the same response. *I will know. I will know. I will know.*" [2]

This book is a real life example of that kind of character right here in Oklahoma. It is just one of many true stories of men and women who met difficult challenges in life with strength and determination, and who made significant contributions to their chosen fields of endeavor. With these remarkable role models, we "…hope it is your destiny, your choice, your achievement, to hear the voice in your own heart, when you face hard decisions in your life, to hear it say to you again and again, until it drowns out every other thought: *I will know. I will know. I will know.*" [3]

DEDICATION

To my family:
Emily for listening,
Claire for encouraging,
Julia for smiling,
and Shelley for everything.
- ED

To daddy, Jerry and Max—three lives well-lived.
Your loyalty honors me; your integrity instructs me;
your honesty anchors me;
and, your unconditional love blesses me—forever.
-JJ

For Isaac and Samuel,
my greatest adventures.
-STS

ACKNOWLEDGMENTS

I must have heard my friend Bob Burke tell the "most amazing rehabilitation story" of Wiley Post a thousand times over the past decade. Though Bob had written nearly twenty books when *From Oklahoma to Eternity* debuted in 1998, this one book seemed to change everything. Calls came from near and far for more stories of unconquerable Oklahomans who made history, right here in our own backyard.

When Bob came to me with the idea of adapting Wiley's story for a younger audience, I knew he would not rest until it was done. I also know Bob first told this story, but I am honored that he gave me the chance to share it once again in a new way.

Thank you to Janice and Sherry, our friend Kyle Flint and my daughter Emily for using their great love for books to help make this one better; my wife Shelley for her heartfelt work during the book's initial production; and we are all thankful to Kris Vculek for her design of the final book.

- Eric

A project of this nature takes on a life of its own; this one was no exception. Over a period of too many months and at different points in the process, significant people provided the necessary support and encouragement that allowed us to see it to completion.

I am honored that Eric asked me to come on board and bring this dream to reality. Because of Bob's award-winning manuscript, we had the opportunity to share Wiley's story with a new generation of young readers. Sherry's artistic gifts brought Wiley to life through her illustrations. Shelley bravely joined the

ACKNOWLEDGMENTS

journey toward design and Emily became our respected junior
editor. My husband and children believed in me and supported
my efforts, and for that, I am blessed. As usual, my best friend,
Tip, provided unconditional encouragement when I needed her
most. Finally, my friends at the Writers' Colony at Dairy Hollow
in Eureka Springs, Arkansas saw to it that my environment was
peaceful and serene, allowing me the focus required to get this
project started. Thanks to Stephen, Cindy, Sandy and the board
for providing this amazing retreat.

- Janice

Thanks to Eric and Janice for trusting me with their words and
giving me the chance to try something new. Thanks to Bob Burke
for shining a light on this amazing man's life and others like him.

- Sherry

INTRODUCTION
A Pioneer Spirit

"What America owes to the men who opened up the West,
aviation will owe to Wiley Post"
—Capt. Edward V. Rickenbacker

With a sixth-grade education, a prison record, and one eye —Wiley Post was a pioneer. Living one of America's greatest success stories, he was a man who exceeded all expectations, overcame his criminal past, and conquered his physical and emotional limitations. With unwavering grit and strength of character, Wiley made his dreams become a reality and flew into aviation history.

As we examine Wiley's life, the skills and behaviors that distinguish him clearly define his character. Captain Edward Rickenbacker, America's leading World War I flying ace, knew Wiley well. After Post's death, a *New York Times* reporter asked him what strengths of character Wiley possessed that made him so exceptional. He replied that Wiley had four qualities that encouraged "his pioneer spirit" and ensured that he would make significant contributions during his lifetime.

"First, he was a natural flyer, a man born with as sensitive a touch as any aviator could develop. His substratosphere flights, in which he shed his landing gear in order to increase his speed…indicate his genius at controlling a plane…that sort of work requires an artist's touch, yet Post did it many times without failing.

Second…stamina…he could take more grueling punishment than any man I ever knew and suffer less from it…after his record-breaking round-the-world flight…he had been awake and flying for 24 hours previous and had not had more than

snatches of sleep during a punishing eight days...[yet] he
seemed no more fatigued than the average man is after
spending a day of routine work at his desk.
Third...He was absolutely fearless and seemed not to have a
nerve in his body.
Finally...He had determination. Nothing could shake him
from what he wanted to do, and he could become at will an
irresistible force or an immovable object. [1]

Another friend and fellow aviator, Amelia Earhart, spoke of Wiley's "simplicity and sincerity of purpose." She described his generosity and willingness to share anything he had learned about planes or motors. Following his death, she wrote:

...Once I asked Wiley why he did not write a book on his
stratosphere flying. "Heck," he said, "there's nothing to write
about. Some people seem to have interesting adventures,
but I never do."...Lost to his friends are his tales of adventures,
told while he denied he had any. [2]

Wiley Post's life is the story of a genuine American hero. Though he was only 36 when he died in Alaska, he had adventures that most can only dream of. Applauded by people everywhere, honored by two Presidents, befriended by the famous, revered by fellow aviators, he still found himself questioning the importance of his life and wondering, "...Is that all there is?"

After accepting the 1999 Oklahoma Book Award for his book about Wiley, Bob Burke reflected upon "one very important thing" he had learned while writing the life story of Wiley Post: "Oklahoma's incredible story always has been about its people".

The remarkable life of Wiley Post is no exception! This is his story...

Wiley, age 6, with his sister Mary. *Courtesy of* The Daily Oklahoman.

THE FUTURE UNFOLDS

"[It] has taken my breath away..."
—Wiley Post

Everyone dreams, but there are a few who dream big. Wiley Post was one who did. Born a farm boy, in the short span of 36 years, he would become a world-renowned aviator, honored by world leaders, revered by fellow pilots, and cheered by millions worldwide. The story of his life is filled with episodes of great risk, remarkable skill, and fierce determination. Aviation experts and enthusiasts agree that the records Wiley set were some of the most remarkable in the history of flight.

Wiley Post was born on November 22, 1898 in a farmhouse near Grand Saline, Texas. When he was four years old, he and his parents and four siblings moved to a farm near Abilene, Texas where another brother was born. Farming played a crucial role in Wiley's development and the Post family bought and sold several small farms. They raised cotton and the Post boys were expected to help. Mr. Post paid them a dime if they picked 100 pounds by the end of the day. At the end of the harvest, the boys were allowed to go to town and spend some of their hard-earned money on "a pocketknife and...slingshot rubber."[1]

With so much land to care for, knowing how to repair equipment and machinery was an essential part of farm life. Wiley's mother reported that, even as a very young child, he was interested in mechanical toys and loved to tinker with things, trying to figure out how they were put together. The mechanical parts of the great harvesters and farm implements always captivated him, and he was good at making sure they worked.

Even though he was born and raised on farms, he somehow knew at a very young age that farm life was not for him, nor was he particularly interested in attending school. Wiley loved the great outdoors, but schoolwork was not easy for him and he often ended up playing instead of studying.

Wiley was quite small for his age and, because of his stocky build, short stature, and lack of formal education, he felt uncomfortable and insecure around people. He often kept to himself and found it difficult to make friends. Instead, he dreamed of great adventures that would make him famous.

He was excited when his parents announced that the family was going to move. Before his birth, Wiley's parents had been farmers in what was then Indian Territory.

It was now 1907 and Mr. Post was eager to move his family back to that area to establish a permanent home. He had heard of new opportunities in the recently formed state of Oklahoma and he could think of little else.

Arriving in Oklahoma, they settled on a farm in the community of Burns. Many years later, Will Rogers, the famous humorist from Oklahoma, would introduce him by saying, "Wiley is an Oklahoman...he did live in Texas as a child, but even Texas children grow up." Throughout their lives both Wiley and Will always were very proud of their Oklahoma heritage.[2]

Wiley's childhood was somewhat unstable, with frequent relocations, financial and emotional insecurity, random educational opportunities, and no real long-term friendships. He enjoyed his life on the farm in rural Oklahoma, but being a strong-willed child he thought his talents were being wasted and he should be able to make his own choices. He disliked the standard school program and his fascination with gadgets and mechanical devices were all that mattered to him.[3]

Though he was only eleven years old at the time, Wiley decided to leave home. As he moved from place to place, he quickly became a local mechanical expert as people sought his help in repairing everything from sewing machines to farm implements. By the age of 13 he had saved enough money to buy a bicycle, the only one for miles around.

On a visit to his parent's farm in Burns in the fall of 1913, Wiley heard about an upcoming fair in Lawton. Little did he know then that this county fair would change his life forever.

He and his older brother Jim decided to make the long, overnight trip to the fair by horse and buggy. When they arrived early the next morning, they enjoyed seeing local farmers' prize livestock and grain exhibits. But it was as the boys prepared to cross the midway to see the displays of the newest farm machinery that something amazing caught Wiley's eye.

There in the open field of the midway was a "queer-looking contraption," the likes of which Wiley had never before seen. They called it an "aeroplane," a Curtis Pusher aeroplane to be

exact. Wiley was fascinated with this strange piece of equipment and spent hours examining it. For the rest of his life, Wiley
declared that he had never seen "a bit of machinery for land, sea,
or sky that [took] my breath away as did that old pusher."[4]

Wiley was amazed as an exhibition pilot described the unusual machine and flew it up into the clear blue Oklahoma sky.
He was so spellbound by the airplane that he forgot to feed and
water their horse.

Over and over again, the local policeman chased Wiley away
from the exhibit. At the end of the day, he crept back to the
plane to look it over just one more time. Wiley quickly forgot his
promise to meet Jim, who looked for him for nearly two hours
before he finally found him sitting quietly in the Pusher's "rickety
seat."[5]

But, Wiley's big day was not over yet. On the trip home from
the fair, a "gas buggy," as they called automobiles at that time,
threw a gritty cloud of dust into the air as it passed the Post boys
and their frightened horse. A few miles up the road they came
upon the car again, only this time it was trapped in the sand by
the side of the road. Hopelessly stuck, the owner of the car tried
to buy their buggy and horse for a dollar, but Wiley had a better
idea. He would take the dollar and bring back help to pull the
car from the ditch in exchange for a ride home. The man agreed,
so Wiley borrowed a team of horses from a nearby sawmill and,
with the help of several mill workers, pulled the car to solid
ground. Having completed his part of the bargain, Wiley was
excited as he climbed into the car and headed for home.

This was a perfect end to what must have felt like the best
day of his life. He had his first encounter with an airplane and

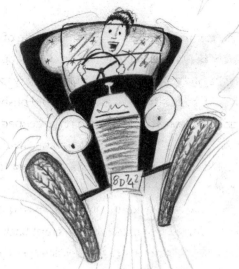

rode in an automobile for the first time. All that in one day! Later, Wiley said the car ride "seemed greater to me" than even a flight around the world. [6]

It was at that county fair in Lawton, Oklahoma in 1913 that Wiley Post discovered his life's purpose. Always fascinated by machinery, here were two new pieces of equipment that could transport people in ways he had never before imagined. He knew that these amazing forms of transportation were "the future and he wanted to be a part of it." [7]

When Wiley was 17, he attended a seven-month auto machinery course in Kansas City, where he graduated as a well-trained chauffeur and mechanic. Because he was now studying things that interested him, he became an outstanding student and explored engineering, mathematics, physics, and chemistry. He read books and studied topics that were not offered in his classes. He never missed a lecture and his test scores were usually at the top of his class. And, he never stopped thinking about airplanes.

Wiley's mother and father at home in Maysville, Oklahoma. *Courtesy of* The Daily Oklahoman.

FALLING AND FLYING

"Any day now…"
—Wiley Post

Working as a driver and grader for a construction company building an airport at Fort Sill, Wiley spent many hours around the airfield hoping that he might be accepted for flight training. He also joined the Students' Army Training Camp during World War I and completed courses in radio communications just as the war was ending. Discharged from the Army, he did not get to use the skills he had acquired…at least not yet!

In the summer of 1919 former military pilots were enchanting the citizens of small towns with acrobatics in their old, battered planes. "Barnstorming" became popular as these pilots would arrive in town and, rather than do any stunts, would fly over the main street at a safe height to not frighten the horses, get the attention of the townspeople, and then sell tickets for plane rides at $5 each. They would make certain that passengers were safely strapped in, then take off and fly around town at several hundred feet.[1]

Wiley paid $25 for a ride in barnstormer Captain Zimmer-man's open-cockpit biplane, but it was a big disappointment. He became a little sick to his stomach, there were no surprising stunts, and he realized that aviators did not "necessarily have those supernatural powers" he had read about in magazine articles.[2]

Wiley's first job following the war was in an oil field site in Walters, Oklahoma. He was only 5'5" and weighed just 130 pounds, but because he was young and strong he was ideally suited for roughneck work in the oil patch. His early days as an expert repairman and his training as an auto mechanic made him especially helpful around the oil rigs.

Wiley was promoted several times and saved his money,

but the gambling fever of "wildcatting" for oil hit him hard. He made a few attempts at staking claims and drilling wells, but all of them failed and left him with no money and no job. Unemployed and bored, Wiley turned to a less respectable way of making money by hijacking cars and robbing his victims.

When he was finally caught by a truckload of hunters, Wiley was convicted of robbery and sentenced to ten years in the State Reformatory at Granite. He began serving his term, but after a few months the prison doctor advised officials that Wiley could not tolerate prison life even though he was physically in good condition, obedient, and respectful. He was severely depressed and doctors believed his condition was "steadily growing worse." [3]

Wiley agreed to a strict release and was paroled. It would be 12 more years before he was granted a full pardon by Governor William H. "Alfalfa Bill" Murray. When Wiley received the pardon in the mail, he could not look at it and forwarded the letter to his parents as an apology for the shame he had caused them. He had learned his lesson the hard way and would never make the same mistake again!

Wiley lived at home with his parents off and on in the early 1920s at their new farm north of Maysville before returning to work in the oil fields. However, the urge to fly was strong and one day, while he was working on a rig near Holdenville, Wiley watched as a plane flew overhead. He was ready to leave the oil business.

Burrell Tibbs' flying circus' Texas Topnotch Fliers were performing in Wewoka, so he decided to apply for a job with them. The only position available was as a parachute jumper and Wiley,

though he had no experience, quickly persuaded Tibbs that
he could do it. He was given a short course in skydiving and
then took his seat in the back of one of the troupe's old, shabby
airplanes.

On the first flight, Wiley forgot everything he had learned
about jumping out of planes. When they reached 2,000 feet,
Tibbs said, "OK. Get ready." Wiley hesitated and could not move
from his seat. He looked back helplessly at Tibbs, but received
nothing more than a scowl from the veteran airman. Wiley
stepped onto the wing and made his way out to the parachute,
which was attached to one of the struts. He buckled the parachute to a harness he was wearing, fell from the wing, found
the release string, and pulled hard. The ground rushed toward
him as the plane raced away above him. With a sudden jerk, the
parachute opened.

Then, for the first time, he looked straight down. As he
landed, his feet stuck in the furrows of the field while the wind
took the parachute ahead of him. He fell flat on his face. It was
not exactly the graceful first landing he had hoped for, but the
experience gave him a great sense of satisfaction, and he felt a
part of the aviation industry at last.[4]

Wiley signed on with the Texas Topnotch Fliers and was
making $50 per jump at weekly air shows in small towns across
Oklahoma. He also received free flight lessons from stunt pilots.

As he learned more and more about the business, Wiley
began setting up his own air shows and scheduled the first stop
on his parachute jumping tour for his family's hometown of
Maysville. He had been using assumed names in his new career

as a parachute jumper, so his parents were shocked when he told them about his upcoming, daring performance. His father, in particular, was not happy about the new job.

Wiley would later remember that particular episode as one of the worst of his aviation career. As he was preparing for the event, he could not find his parachute! He looked everywhere, but never saw it again. Suspiciously, Wiley's father was not at all worried about its disappearance.

Wiley promised the Maysville officials that nothing would stop him from jumping the next Sunday. That week, he traveled by train to Oklahoma City and borrowed a parachute from a friend. The following Sunday, the show began with a few loops and rolls of the plane. The jump went well and even Mr. Post admitted he was proud of his son. Wiley Post was a hero in his own hometown!

Always ready to thrill a crowd with his daredevil stunts, Wiley was very successful as a parachute jumper. He often would wait until the last moment to open his parachute, sometimes using two parachutes. [5]

With more than 100 jumps, he had only one embarrassing incident. While free falling to a meadow that was clear when he previously inspected it, Wiley spotted a mule right where he was to land. As he hit the ground, his parachute floated down over the mule's head. Terrified, the animal turned and ran away, dragging Wiley behind him. It was not the stunt he had planned!

Never one to take a lot of time once he had his mind made up about something, a somewhat overconfident Wiley had only logged about four hours of supervised flight when he decided that it was time to fly solo. After making a $200 deposit for the use of a plane, Wiley started the engine and was in the air in no time. He later admitted that when he realized he was all alone in the plane, he was scared.

He flew around for nearly half an hour before attempting to land. When he cut the power and started down, he forgot to clear the motor out and the engine began to sputter. He pushed the throttle forward and, with some hesitation, the engine caught again. Unfortunately, he neglected to pull the nose up soon enough and was rapidly diving toward the ground. Pulling the plane up at the last moment, Wiley circled the field before making a safe landing. Only later did he discover that he had barely missed hitting a tree on the first landing attempt. The plane's owner, thinking the whole thing was a stunt and that Wiley was just showing off, gave Wiley back the $200 deposit in full. He was now a real pilot! [6]

Wiley was convinced that he must own his own airplane. He knew that unless he did he would never be able to log enough flight hours to become a commercial aviator, which was his goal.

Halfheartedly, he returned to work as a driller, determined to stay in the fields only as long as it took to save the money he would need to buy a plane. He told anyone who would listen that he would soon have a plane of his own. He never could have imagined the events that were about to completely change his life.

THE EYE

"Wiley just grinned…"
—Powell Briscoe

On October 1, 1926, Wiley was at work on an oil rig near Seminole, Oklahoma when another worker struck an iron bolt with a sledgehammer. A chip broke off the bolt and landed in Wiley's left eye. The local doctor tried to save it, but a massive infection developed and he began to lose sight in both eyes. Fearing blindness, Wiley agreed to allow the doctors to remove his left eye with the hope that the infection would improve in his right eye.

At just 27 years old, Wiley had only one eye, was an ex-convict with a sixth-grade education, and had almost no formal flight training. The odds were against him, but Wiley had no intention of giving up.

During the 1920s, the excitement of aviation in America was everywhere. Charles Lindbergh flew solo across the Atlantic Ocean and airmail routes were opening across the continent. Wiley knew that somehow he could overcome his misfortune and become part of the excitement. As was typical of him, Wiley saw this as one more challenge he had to conquer.

After his eye was removed, Wiley recovered at his uncle's home in southwest Texas, where he practiced gauging his depth perception by looking at distant hills and trees. He would guess how far away they were and then step off the distance to check his accuracy. He knew depth perception would be required of a skilled pilot and would be important to him in the future. Two months later, he could judge distances better than before the accident. He also learned to land a plane by using the height of telephone poles and two-story buildings.

Because he was hurt at work, Wiley was awarded $1,800 for the loss of his eye. After paying expenses, he had more than $1,200 left and spent $240 of it for a slightly damaged Canuck airplane. After spending another $300 for repairs, he was ready for business and painted the word "Post" below the rear cockpit. Around this time, Wiley also began wearing a patch over his eye, a symbol that would later make him easily recognizable all over the world.

Wiley purchased his plane, took two hours worth of flying lessons, and opened his business as a flight instructor. He also worked in flying circuses and for oilmen who needed to use airplanes to get to their leases quickly. Anyone who had the money and needed to get somewhere in a hurry could hire Wiley and his plane. He became adept at flying in the rough country of southeast Oklahoma, southern Arkansas, and northeast Texas where the scrubby timber made emergency landings almost impossible. There always was fog and bad air currents, but Wiley became an expert at navigating through the difficult terrain. He was known for his ability to find a landing area in places that

other pilots would not use, earning himself the reputation as part daredevil and part gifted pilot.[1]

In 1927, Wiley was in Sweetwater, Texas when he visited 17-year-old Mae Laine, which he described as his "first thrill aside from aviation." His aviation business began to suffer when he turned down weekend flying jobs so he could fly to Sweetwater to see Mae. When they spoke of marriage, Mae's parents strongly objected. But Wiley was never one to quit, so he and Mae decided to elope.

They left Sweetwater in Wiley's $240 plane that had worked

perfectly for more than 800 hours in the air. But on that particular night the engine quit and Wiley was forced to land the plane with a smack on the rough ground of a recently harvested cornfield.

After fixing the engine, Wiley and Mae were married by a local minister. After that, the newlyweds removed the corn shocks from their runway in the cornfield and resumed the flight.

It was during this period that Wiley gave flying lessons to aspiring pilots such as Eula "Pearl" Carter-Scott, a 12-year-old girl who often watched Wiley land in her father's pasture near Marlow. Pearl could not stop asking Wiley about planes and flying. When he finally took her up, he asked if she wanted to hold the stick. She told him, "of course," and flew the plane for quite a while. It was her first flying lesson. She became so excited about flying that she talked her father into buying her a monoplane. Pearl's father, George, had been Wiley's first paying passenger and, because he was blind, felt a special connection with the one-eyed pilot.

Wiley picked out a plane for Pearl, and as soon as a landing field and hangar were ready, he flew it to her home in Marlow. From her classroom she could hear the engine flying over the school and was thrilled to find both her father and Wiley in the principal's office to deliver her plane. Pearl went on to fly solo in 1928 and was named the youngest female aviator in the United States. [2]

Later that year, a major financial setback came when Wiley seriously damaged his plane on a hunting trip in Mexico. He brought the plane back home but did not have enough money to pay the repair bill and had to sell it.

Wiley and Mae moved to Purcell, but barnstorming jobs were

hard to find by the winter of 1927. Money was scarce and Wiley went looking for a job. He heard about two Chickasha oilmen, F.C. Hall and Powell Briscoe, who wanted to use an airplane in their oil business and were looking for a good pilot. Wiley had flown so many barnstorming tours that he did not need a map to fly Oklahoma's oil country. He desperately wanted the job, and returned to Mr. Hall's office several days in a row before Mr. Hall agreed to see him. There were other applicants for the position, but the wealthy oilmen were impressed with Wiley and gave him the job. [3]

Wiley enjoyed his work and became close friends with the two businessmen. The three men made a great team in the difficult business of oil drilling and leasing. Eventually Hall, who seemed to be a born gambler and risk taker, became like a second father to Wiley. Mr. Briscoe also was quite close to Wiley and appreciated his bravery, saying that Wiley "didn't have a nerve in his body. When other people were scared, Wiley just grinned." [4]

With a secure job and more money coming in, things were looking up for Wiley and Mae Post. However, Congress passed a new aeronautics law that caused Wiley to worry about his future in the flying business. One particular section in the new law required that pilots have vision of not less than 20/30 in each eye, although it stated in certain instances exceptions might be accepted. The code prohibited giving a pilot license to anyone with "organic disease of the eye, ear, nose or throat." [5]

As he dodged inspectors at major airports, he knew avoiding detection would not work forever. It was just a matter of time before he would have to have a license to continue working in aviation.

After Wiley discovered a loophole in the new law that provided for exceptions that could be granted to experienced aviators with physical defects, he passed an Aeronautics Board test
and flew 700 probationary hours before he was finally licensed
as a pilot on September 16, 1928. Orville Wright, the very person
who was at the controls of the first human flight at Kitty Hawk,
North Carolina on December 17, 1903, signed his license. Wiley
Post was officially ready for a great adventure!

Wiley's pilot's license. *Courtesy of Oklahoma Historical Society.*

THE WINNIE MAE

"It seemed to anticipate my moves..."
—Wiley Post

Late in 1928, F.C. Hall sent Wiley to the Lockheed Aircraft Company's factory in Burbank, California to exchange their open-cockpit plane for a new closed-cabin Lockheed Vega plane. The new design was a major change from the planes that Wiley had previously flown. The most modern airplane of 1928, Wiley knew it was one of those airplanes that could open up all kinds of new possibilities for him.

Named after F.C. Hall's daughter, the *Winnie Mae* was a trend-setting plane that featured a plywood body with the wing supports and control cables hidden from view.

Interestingly, the name "Mae" played a major role in Wiley's life. His mother, his wife, and his favorite airplane all were named Mae.

Upon the return flight home to Oklahoma City, Wiley was impressed with the improved ride offered by the enclosed-cockpit of the sleek new aircraft. He said, "...I had more pleasure test-flying that airplane than any of the dozens I have initiated to the air since...sitting at the stick behind that Wasp was like changing

from a slow freight to a limited express. It was so sensitive and re-sponsive to the controls that it seemed to anticipate my moves."[1]

Everything was going well for Hall and Briscoe in the oil busi-ness and for Wiley in the aviation business. Then, the shock of the Great Depression hit Oklahoma. The state suffered through severe dust storms and all 77 counties in Oklahoma were desig-nated disaster areas.[2]

As their oil investments dried up, Hall and Briscoe could not afford to pay Wiley's salary or cover the costs of owning an airplane, so the decision was made to sell the *Winnie Mae* back to the Lockheed Aircraft Company. The name was painted over and Wiley sadly flew her farewell flight back to California. Once again, Wiley was without a job.

The airline industry was in its infancy at the time and seri-ously affected by the Great Depression. During this time, the American public demanded adventurous deeds that entertained and distracted them from the trauma of their lives.

In these early years of aviation, many young pilots sought

publicity by trying to set long-distance-flight records and were
sometimes offered large sums of money for extremely hazard-
ous flights. One such event was Charles Lindbergh's flight from
New York to Paris in a tiny monoplane plane named *The Spirit of
St. Louis*. International acclaim would accompany the $25,000
prize. Prior to Lindbergh's flight, several lives had been lost in the
effort to win the prize. At the age of 25, following a 3,610-mile,
34-hour flight across the Atlantic, Colonel Lindbergh became an
international hero.

Desperate for work, Wiley was hired to become a Lockheed
test pilot in California. Such an exciting, high-risk job allowed
Wiley to learn all about aircraft design and flight-test procedures
from the country's best aeronautical engineers and pilots.

In June of 1930, the oil business was improving and F.C. Hall
was ready to buy another airplane. He offered Wiley his old pilot-
ing job and Wiley gladly accepted. He was ready to come home
to Oklahoma!

Flying Hall's new $22,000, seven-passenger Lockheed Vega
monoplane, once again named *Winnie Mae*, was a dream come
true. Known for its airworthiness and rugged dependability, the
Vega was one of the most famous record-breaking airplanes of
the 1930s. Indeed, the most notable accomplishments of Wiley's
aviation career were achieved using this aircraft.

Traveling home in style, Wiley left Los Angeles with his wife
Mae beside him and returned to Oklahoma City.[3] Wiley enjoyed being back home in Oklahoma and dreamed of setting
a transcontinental flying record of some kind. He said, "With a
light heart I resumed my old duties…Oklahoma and the people
I knew so well looked good to me…I hardly got going, however,

when the old desire to make a record flight took a tight hold on me again."[4]

With the approval of his boss, Wiley entered the *Winnie Mae* in a non-stop air race derby between Los Angeles and Chicago, Illinois. He felt his plane was speedy enough to win, but he made several changes to the ship to make it even faster. He asked Harold Gatty, a flight navigator living in California, to plan the 1,760-mile course between the two great cities.

Gatty worked all night before the start of the race and handed maps and charts to Wiley just before take off. The race also had attracted four of the finest pilots in the country. Wiley, who had never before used maps and charts during a flight, won the $7,500 prize, and said, "Gatty's charts led me straight over the course, and my tail was being pushed by a good wind…my compass started swinging. Then it stuck…I had to navigate from the map. The misfortune made me lose about 40 minutes…Even then, I still beat my nearest rival of the day into the field by 11 seconds." The new *Winnie Mae* averaged 192 miles per hour, and set a new speed record of nine hours, nine minutes, and four seconds. [5]

When Wiley, "…nonchalantly walked to check in, the judges had to consult their program to see who this portly, bushy-haired fellow was." The outcome was a surprise to everyone but Wiley! [6]

Wiley was excited to win the derby, but was even more thrilled when he looked up to see a plane flash across the finish line, taking second place. She had been repainted, slightly altered, and had a new boss, but there she was, the old *Winnie Mae*, and she was as good as ever. [7]

Having set a new speed record over the continental United States, Wiley was one step closer to making his biggest dream come true. . .he wanted to fly around the world.

As Mae watches, Wiley traces his flight around the earth. *Courtesy of* The Daily Oklahoman.

GET READY...GET SET

"That phrase 'going around the world' had a great thrill for me..."
—Wiley Post

Elaborate networks of airlines covered the nation, but air travel needed something unique to encourage passenger business. There was still concern about the dangers of flying and the public needed reassurance about the safety of aircraft under all kinds of conditions. Wiley knew that if one was cautious and had a reasonable amount of experience, there was absolutely nothing to fear about flight. He wanted to demonstrate that airplanes could not only be faster, but also safer than any other form of available transportation. He had "something original" in mind that would get the attention of the public and reassure them airplane travel was safe. [1]

Though Wiley was famous after winning the race in Chicago, he was unaccustomed to the attention. His insecurities about his size, education, and criminal past haunted him. What he did not realize at the time was that he was about to receive a lot more attention!

It was late 1930 and, with the new interest in aviation, cross-country flying had lost its excitement for Wiley. He wanted to do something that had never been done before, and flying around the world was something he had wanted to do since he was a young boy:

> I still get a kick out of my old history book, which shows a picture of Columbus looking out to sea. Columbus thought he was going around the world to Asia, and just that phrase "going around the world" had a great thrill for me, especially as my view of the world was the flat horizon of Texas.[2]

F.C. Hall was again suffering financially because of the Great Depression and did not need a full-time pilot. He gave Wiley permission to use his free time to prepare for an around the world flight in the *Winnie Mae*, under two conditions. First, Mae would have to agree that Wiley could make the flight. In case of an accident, he did not want people to believe that the plans had been made without Mrs. Post's knowledge. And second, Wiley had to complete the flight with no commercial support. Hall told him that the profits from the flight would be used to pay expenses and Wiley would have to "hope for a surplus" to cover payment for his services. He was not allowed to personally endorse any equipment or merchandise until after the flight was successfully completed and his agreement with Hall fulfilled. Wiley agreed to each condition, though he knew that without commercial backing his flight preparations would involve more personal time and labor and result in several delays. [3]

Wiley planned a flight that would take him east to west around the globe, from New York and back again in ten days— something that had never been done before in aviation history. His equipment would consist of one airplane, "the fastest load-carrier" he had ever seen, the *Winnie Mae*. Wiley saved several thousand dollars to use for the trip, and left the rest of the business planning to Hall.

He knew he would have to have a top-notch navigator if he was to be successful in this record-setting attempt. Wiley knew that Harold Gatty was his man.

In mid-January, 1931, Wiley flew the *Winnie Mae* to Los Angeles to ask Harold Gatty to help prepare the route and keep him on course during the flight. Reluctantly, Gatty agreed to participate because he had several theories about aerial navigation that he was eager to try.

Although he was three years younger than Wiley, Harold Gatty had many years of experience as a navigator and was a well-respected pilot. He was an Australian naval cadet who invented the ground speed and drift indicator that ultimately became the basis of the automatic pilot, an instrument that forever changed the field of aviation.

As Gatty carefully prepared an around-the-world flight plan, Wiley devoted his time to the practical engineering and mechanical needs of the flight. He knew that he would have to begin training his body and his mind for the difficult flight ahead of him. As Wiley flew about the country in the regular routine of his job, he tried his best to keep his mind clear so he could pilot the aircraft automatically, without mental effort, "letting my actions be wholly controlled by my subconscious."[4]

He changed his hours of sleep every day for months to prepare himself to sleep only at available times to avoid severe fatigue during the long flight. Wiley found that by limiting his intake of food he did not require as much sleep.

In January, 1931, Wiley and Mae left Chickasha to return to the Lockheed factory in Los Angeles. As each month of preparation passed, Wiley found more ways to streamline the *Winnie Mae* and reduce its weight. He modified the cockpit and replaced the straight-backed, steel pilot's seat with a "nice armchair… [that] was a trifle short for leg room perhaps, but quite restful." He would need to be able to shift positions during the long hours of the flight without being too far from the controls, so a comfortable chair was a necessity. [5]

Because of the long flight, additional fuel tanks were attached at the sides and top of the body of the plane, requiring Wiley to enter the cockpit through a trap door in the roof of the cabin. Because of the design changes, he was completely cut off from the rear compartment, where Gatty would be sitting during the flight.

Jimmy Doolittle, the famous aerobatic and fighter pilot who pioneered instrument flying, suggested grouping the flying instruments to best accommodate Wiley's good eye and other senses. Wiley knew instrument readings would allow him to "fly blind" in total darkness or in clouds. [6]

Gatty worked night and day drafting charts and plotting courses for the entire flight. His seat in the rear compartment was moveable so that he could shift his weight forward or backward for proper weight distribution as fuel was burned. He even designed a special speaking tube so he could talk with Wiley during the flight. If the engine noise became too loud to hear their voices, a wire could be used to pull notes through the tube.

A hatch was installed in the top of the fuselage to allow Gatty to make frequent celestial readings. Another was at his feet where he could calculate the drift and air speed of the plane. Nothing was left to chance. [7]

As Wiley and Gatty finalized the technical aspects of the flight, they began working on the political concerns of making a trip around the world by visiting the embassies of many countries. The United States had not yet recognized Russia as a country, so no American flyer was officially permitted to touch down there. They would need at least unofficial permission from Russian officials to land the *Winnie Mae* in their country. Without it, they would not be able to use the route they had carefully planned. The U.S.S.R. gave them their assurance that they would not prevent them from making their flight, but they could not give them any official recognition.

F.C. Hall knew that there was money to be made from the flight. Wiley and Gatty were to take autographed envelopes to postmark as they landed in each country, and then sell them when they returned home. In addition, exclusive rights to daily coverage of the flight were sold to the *New York Times*, which promised its readers "a real scoop" in aviation history. Hall also signed an agreement with a newsreel service that provided Gatty with a motion picture camera and boxes of film that he would use to record the historic flight. [8]

On May 23, 1931, Wiley and Gatty landed at Roosevelt Field in New York and made the final preparations for their 15,000-mile flight that would take them over the North Atlantic, to Berlin and Moscow, over Siberia, across the Bering Strait to Alaska, then to

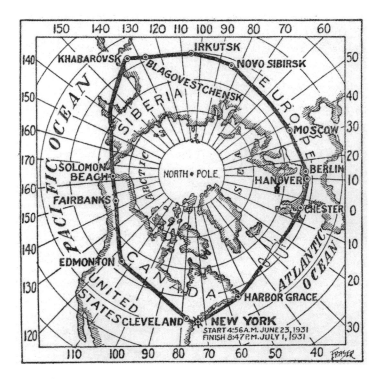

Canada and back to New York.

The world was taking notice of the pending record-setting adventure and one reporter compared the flight to the 1872 adventure novel by Jules Verne, *Around the World in 80 Days*. "Jules Verne sent mythical Phileas Fogg around the world in 80 days. Two hardy fliers hope to make the trip in one tenth, or maybe one-eighth of the time." [9]

Though Wiley and Gatty openly announced that they would be happy with a new world record of ten days, the men really wanted to complete the trip in just seven or eight. However, they would have to get off the ground first!

Weeks went by as Wiley and Gatty waited for weather conditions to improve across the Atlantic Ocean. At the slightest glimpse of better weather, the pair would gather their gear and sit on the runway, only to be disappointed when the bad conditions continued.

Wiley met daily with Dr. James K. Kimball, a United States Weather Bureau meteorologist in New York City. Pilots frequently wanted his approval to take off in less-than-favorable conditions, and Wiley was no exception. However, Kimball was confident in his forecast of bad weather 1,000 miles out over the Atlantic and delayed the departure of the historic flight. Wiley and Gatty tried to convince Kimball to give them the go-ahead based upon Wiley's proven ability to fly through fog and clouds. He simply rejected their pleas saying that "the weather must improve sooner or later." [10]

Their frustration was mounting with every delay. Finally, in the early morning hours of June 23—one month after they had arrived—the weather cleared over the Atlantic, but not at the airport in New York. It was still raining! Gatty was anxious and excited, but Wiley was his usual relaxed self. Gatty said:

Calm old Wiley! He plunged through the rain in a borrowed raincoat...The zero hour came...Then Wiley used his head. With that rain it would have been impossible to be sure on the take off. Looking through the diamond-like drops on the windshield at the brilliant lights of the airport would distort everything. He refused to risk our months of effort on a few drops of rain and a few seconds of rushing along the ground at 70 miles an hour. [11]

Wiley decided to postpone take-off until dawn. When day-light came, the rain was worse than before; but, without having to deal with the glare of the runway lights, Wiley knew that they could now taxi safely. They were finally ready and they were not going to waste another minute.

Gatty settled into his chair as Wiley shouted, "Gas on; switch off." The *Winnie Mae* burst to life.

Shortly after take-off, Harold Gatty began to write the first of many entries into the flight log, "Tuesday, June 23, 8:55:21. Took off 4:55 daylight-saving time, set course 63 degrees, visibility poor." [12]

Wiley's dream of breaking a world aviation record was now coming true, and the *Winnie Mae* was carrying him on an historic voyage around the world!

GO!

"I'll be tickled to death if you can tell us where we are…"
—Wiley Post

Wiley spotted the airfield at Harbor Grace, Newfoundland six hours and 47 minutes into their flight around the world. A small group of photographers and curious townspeople watched as the *Winnie Mae* circled the airfield before landing. Wiley said, "Get as far back as you can, kid," and Gatty scooted toward the tail of the plane. As the nose drifted up, the fliers settled in for a perfect landing.

Wiley and Gatty were ready to stretch their legs and hurriedly enjoyed a home cooked meal before asking their hosts to take them back to the airport. Completely focused upon his journey around the world, Wiley did not have time to get hungry. He carried a bottle of tomato juice and a few cookies along, but never ate the three sandwiches he had hidden under his seat.

At this point, Gatty realized that he had left his billfold back at the New York hotel. All he had in his pocket was $1, which was not very much for the long trip they had planned. He immediately spent it on food, and from that point on, both men had to rely on the $34 that Wiley brought with him for their personal expenses.

Gatty began calculating the next leg of the trip, using the tail of the airplane for a table. This particular portion of the flight over the ocean was important to Gatty because it would allow him to test some of his navigational theories and strengthen his professional reputation.

Observing Wiley's preflight inspection of the plane, Gatty was indeed impressed. He described him as, "…the most amazing person. Within sight of the *Winnie Mae*, he became a different man. I shall always remember his moves at Harbor Grace as one of the highlights of the race. Despite his calmness, I have never seen him so meticulous." Gatty later described the process:

> *With maddening thoroughness he moved about, but the precision of his movements inspired confidence in me as I watched. Not a motion was wasted and not a square inch of the vital parts of the* Winnie Mae *escaped his inspection. With borrowed pliers he tightened fuel couplings, tested vents, and got oil all over himself, so that he looked like a "grease-monkey" when he finally stood on the spat of the*

*wheel for a last pose in front of the…photographers. Then
his head disappeared into the cockpit, and he started the
engine.* [1]

Satisfied that his plane was working well, Wiley was ready
to take off. When he nodded that everything was ready, Gatty
scrambled to his seat in the rear of the plane and later said, "The
biggest moment of my life had arrived. I was about to fly over
the ocean. I could not but think what my former shipmates
would say about my idea of crossing the Atlantic in one night." [2]

For the *Winnie Mae*, nearly 2,000 miles of nothing but ocean
lay ahead. Gatty's navigational skills and the location of the stars,
sun, and moon were their only tools to determine where they
were. Almost immediately after take-off, Gatty saw something
that concerned him:

*A bit of white, like steam, floated above the headland and
stood out against the brown cliff. Fog, low hanging! It
looked as if we were on the edge of a low-pressure area.
I knew we were in for it, but I had not expected it so soon.* [3]

Because they had delayed their flight in the hopes of good
weather over the Atlantic, this was a major disappointment.
They found themselves flying through heavy fog, while thick
clouds hid both the moon and ocean.

Once, while climbing in altitude to avoid a heavy rainstorm,
the air speed indicator took a sudden drop and it felt as if the
ship were about to get away from Wiley.

Gatty yelled, "Hey!"

Wiley responded, "Hey. What?"

By that time the indicator had returned to normal and Gatty
responded, "Oh nothing. Just keep on dead ahead."

Irritated, Wiley did not want to be unnecessarily bothered and said, "Wait 'til we get out of this soup, and then I'll be tickled to death if you can tell us where we are."

The inability to see where they were going was a huge concern, but there was another issue that worried Gatty. One of the standard procedures of long-distance pilots was the practice of completely draining a fuel tank before switching to another. When a tank was emptied, the engine would sputter, cough, and nearly stall until the pilot switched to a full tank. A person unaccustomed to this procedure would fear the worst. Though Gatty became familiar with the process, it continued to alarm him throughout the flight. He asked Wiley to let him know in advance when a tank was running low so that he could prepare himself for the ordeal.

To escape the fog, they climbed in altitude, but nothing helped. For the rest of the night Wiley held to his course, and from time to time Gatty would simply tell him, "A little more to the right, a little more to the left." On they flew, "…through that misty grayness. We were swallowed up as it closed in behind. No sign of life, no guide to our path." [4]

Finally, after calculating their speed and the number of hours they had been in the air, both men felt that they surely must be over land. They decided to descend through the clouds to see if they were right. For 20 minutes they went down in altitude, unable to see anything in their path. Finally, Gatty, who could only see below and behind the plane, shouted through the tube, "Water!" Wiley, looking out the front of the plane could see something that was blocked from Gatty's view. He shouted, "Land!" [5]

They spotted an airfield and decided to land, not knowing for sure where they were. Four men in uniforms raced toward the aircraft, identifying themselves as Royal Air Force (RAF) men. Wiley had landed the *Winnie Mae* at the Royal Air Force's Sealand Airdrome, near Liverpool, England. They had crossed the Atlantic in 16 hours and 17 minutes, a new record for crossing the Atlantic Ocean.

Exhausted, Wiley had no idea where they had landed, he just knew that he had found land, and that was good enough for him. When he tried to speak, he could not hear the sound of his own voice because the roar of the engine was still in his ears. He was temporarily deaf.

Wiley and Gatty were eager to set off for their next stop in Berlin, but the RAF insisted that the men stay for lunch while the plane was serviced. The British mechanics figured exactly how much gas it would take to get to Berlin and filled the tanks accordingly. Wiley let them know he did not want any unnecessary fuel to add to the weight of his plane. They also received detailed maps for their course to Berlin.

Because he was so tired on this leg of the trip, Wiley had trouble staying on course, which caused him to use more fuel than he had calculated. He had to land in Hannover, Germany to determine their exact location and get directions to the Tempelhof airport near Berlin. Again, fatigue was a factor when both he and Gatty forgot to check their fuel supply while they were on the ground. After they took off, they realized that their fuel was too low to fly all the way to Berlin, so they returned to Hannover to refuel. Wiley later admitted all he wanted to do was reach

Berlin and sleep. He was exhausted. [6]

Wiley was eager to land at Tempelhof airport because it was built adjacent to the center of Berlin. He said, "I was impressed with the nearness of the airport to the big squares in the town… Even out in roomy Oklahoma we can't seem to get the airports so close to town." [7]

Large crowds awaited their arrival in Berlin and, though hungry and tired, Wiley and Gatty quickly realized that a hero's welcome had been prepared for them. As the men sat down to an extravagant meal, reporters began asking questions. Wiley did not speak German, so he could not understand their questions, and the reporters did not speak English, so they were unable to understand his answers. After a few frustrating attempts to communicate, they left him alone and Wiley breathed a sigh of relief.

The next morning, Wiley and Gatty checked the weather reports hoping for an improvement over what they had thus far experienced. It was not to be. The forecast indicated that rain, fog, and low visibility would trouble them over much of the Russian state. [8]

It was on this leg of the flight that the *Winnie Mae* encountered a storm so severe Wiley could barely see beyond the plane's propeller. He was sometimes forced to fly at an altitude of only 400 feet. Many times he would have to pull up sharply to avoid hitting the smoke stacks of buildings.

Shortly after crossing into Russia, the fliers experienced the worst weather of the trip. Without warning, they encountered a rainstorm, "…like a Kansas cloudburst." Wiley later said he had never seen rain run so thick on a flying airplane:

Worse than all else, I couldn't see. Not seeing here was much worse than it was over the ocean. There we had plenty of altitude and nothing to hit, but hedgehopping through Russia with about 200 yards visibility and 100 or more miles an hour speed is enough to make your hair stand on end every time you cross a fence. [9]

Finally, the rain stopped as the Moscow runway came into view. The landing was uneventful and quiet compared to their previous landings because the newspapers had barely mentioned the flight.

After landing, they had to quickly clean up and get ready for another nine-course dinner in their honor. They were toasted with champagne, just as they had been in Berlin, but once again requested only water to drink. They would not compromise the success of their trip by dulling their senses with alcohol. The elaborate dinner lasted until 11 o'clock. Because the sun rose at 2:00 a.m. that time of year, Wiley left a wake-up call for 1:00 a.m., allowing just two hours sleep. They returned to the airport to prepare the *Winnie Mae* for the long flight across southern Siberia.

Even though the landing in Moscow had been easy, the take-off was much more complicated. A major delay occurred when the tanks were filled with Russian Imperial gallons of fuel rather than United States gallons, as Wiley had requested. The extra weight would make it dangerous to take off, so they had to wait while mechanics removed gas from one of the tanks. Knowing they had 2,600 miles to cover, Wiley was concerned that if they did not get off quickly he would have to finish the next leg of the flight in darkness.

Wiley was upset at the delay and told the workers so. Of course, they did not speak English, so they had no idea what he was saying. Gatty was afraid that Wiley was so upset he would wear himself out before they got back in the air. Finally, he and Wiley finished removing the excess fuel themselves.

Once the fuel levels had been corrected, Wiley started the engines and yelled, "Let's go kid," and "like a frightened colt, *Winnie Mae* increased her usual steady lope to a wild gallop, as she ripped a hole through the Soviet air." [10]

By the time the fliers had reached Moscow, Gatty had begun to grow attached to the *Winnie Mae*. After experiencing what she could do in flight, he began to understand why Wiley's mood seemed to change whenever he approached the ship. She was an amazing plane, and he appreciated her more every day.

Gatty had been given maps in Moscow, but soon discovered that they were full of inaccuracies. Not until decades later was it admitted that the maps had been deliberately falsified to avoid assisting the country's enemies with accurate information.

The *Winnie Mae* was a small aircraft and on long legs of the flight the fliers had trained themselves to eat light meals to reduce the fatigue factor and resolve the problem of not having a restroom on board. If they had to relieve themselves, they simply used a wax-coated ice cream carton with a lid and then tossed it overboard when they were over water. [11]

Because of the delayed take-off, the limited amount of sleep, and the long banquets, both men were plagued with fatigue and slowed reactions. They agreed to land at Novosibirsk to spend the night rather than go all the way to Irkutsk. They felt that a full night's sleep would help them make up the extra mileage on

the next leg of the trip.

At Novosibirsk, they were escorted into town to a hotel, which provided them a room on the fifth floor. However, there was no elevator. The exhausted fliers climbed the stairs to their room to discover that there were no bathroom facilities or running water. They were too exhausted to care about their accommodations at that point and had just flopped down on the bed when someone knocked on the door to inform them that yet another banquet had been arranged in their honor. Wiley wanted to refuse the offer, but it would have been considered an insult. Bone weary with fatigue, they went back down the stairs and walked to a nearby restaurant, where "...the quality of the meal turned out to be first class and favorably comparable to top western restaurants." [12]

Wiley and Gatty enjoyed the banquet and a few hours of sleep before the trip back to the airport. Wiley was so exhausted that he slept in his clothes on the hard bed. Unfortunately, Gatty had to contend with bedbugs and spent most of the night scratching, waking up with welts all over his face.

On the way back down the stairs the next morning, Wiley missed the last step and sprained his ankle. For him, this could be a serious injury because a pilot used his feet to control the rudder. Neither was about to let these problems slow them down; they had a 20-hour flight ahead of them. [13]

The fliers carried no luggage on the trip and quickly returned to the air as they headed toward the Russian city of Irkutsk, six hours away. After suffering through his bedbug incident, Wiley suggested that Gatty catch up on his sleep. He knew he would be able to navigate through the rain by following the rail lines while Gatty was resting. When Irkutsk came into view, Wiley shook the plane to wake up his navigator so that Gatty could shift his weight to the tail section for landing. [14]

Wiley said that at that moment, there was nothing in the world that mattered to him but the "good old *Winnie Mae* and her trusty motor, Gatty, and a few scrubby fields." Though there was a bit of jovial bickering between the two, his appreciation for Gatty grew throughout the long trip:

Gatty was a good passenger, one of the best I ever carried.
He never asked any questions or raised any disturbance
about the way I pulled that ship up or knocked it down in
dives that I know must have plugged his ears. [15]

HALF WAY THERE

"…hang on!"
—Wiley Post

The largest crowd since Berlin met the plane when it landed in Irkutsk. They were there for only two hours. Wiley sent a brief cable to the *New York Times*, "We are now half way around the world in three days and twenty hours. Our physical condition is perfect and we are continuing immediately for Blagoveshchensk." He sent a two-word cable to Mae that said, "Feeling fine." [1]

It had been raining all day in Blagoveshchensk and two inches of water covered the airfield. Wiley saw the lights of the airport, which, in the rain, looked as though they were sitting on top of a lake. There was not much Wiley could do but feel his way to the ground and trust his luck. He yelled to Gatty, "Get as far back as you can! Hold your instruments so they won't break! Set yourself for a jolt and hang on!" [2]

As the plane touched down, mud sprayed across the windshield. When Wiley tried to turn, the *Winnie Mae's* left wheel began to sink. They were hopelessly bogged down in the mud. Wiley felt his heart sink along with the wheel. He feared that his life-long dream was going to end in a mud hole in Siberia. [3]

Several people waded out to help. Two Danish telegraph operators attached a rope to an old Ford and tried to pull the *Winnie Mae* from the sludge. The wheels of the car spun furiously, throwing mud in every direction, but only accomplished sinking the plane deeper into the earth.

Wiley and Gatty were understandably upset, but a Danish airport official finally announced that he had sent for some laborers and a tractor that would arrive by morning to free the plane from the mud. Both men were soaking wet and covered in mud. Gatty later described the situation by saying, "There is no denying they were low hours for both of us." After much persuasion, Gatty decided to abandon the ship and headed for a bath and dinner at a nearby home. [4]

Wiley decided to stay with the *Winnie Mae*. He was concerned that the plane be properly attached to the tractor and that it be refueled correctly, and fell asleep in Gatty's chair in the back of the plane to await the arrival of the tractor.

When daylight arrived and the tractor still had not appeared, Wiley decided horses would once again come to his rescue as they had years before when he was a boy pulling an automobile out of the ditch. He persuaded a local farmer to bring his plow horses and, along with a dozen men with ropes, freed the plane from the deep mud hole.

It was their last chance to get out of Siberia and they would waste no more time. Wiley and Gatty jumped in the plane and took off; they already had lost 12 hours, and were more than ready to continue their journey.

Finally in the air, they made their way to Khabarovsk, the last stop in Russia. Wiley knew the *Winnie Mae* desperately needed servicing before attempting the most demanding part of the trip to Solomon, Alaska. It would be a very difficult route filled with dangerous over-water flying, fog, and unknown mountain peaks, and he had to do something to improve her condition before asking so much of her. Wiley began by going to work on "the old girl's heart." [5]

Wiley replaced four spark plugs and Gatty collected weather data, studying his charts and maps for the best route to Alaska. They agreed to three hours of sleep at a local hotel before returning to the airfield, where the wind was blowing straight across the runway. It would be impossible for the *Winnie Mae* to take off with a full load of fuel. Deciding the risk was too great, Wiley and Gatty found two cots in a hangar at the airfield and slept until the next afternoon. When they awoke, wind conditions had changed and they wasted no time getting in the air. Amazingly, Wiley felt the *Winnie Mae* "...flew off in better shape than she had at Harbor Grace," when the flight began. [6]

As Wiley had anticipated, the flight to Solomon was long and dangerous. They had to begin by flying just 75 feet off the water in order to improve their time against a slight head wind. They flew so low that the trees skimmed just under the wheels. The sight of the *Winnie Mae* so close to the water frightened the natives, who never before had seen or heard an airplane, as they paddled their sampans on the Amur River. Wiley later said, "Despite the work of flying the ship for hours so low that it had to be 'flown every second' along the way, I was not the least bit tired." [7]

At this point in the flight, Wiley and Gatty had to make a tough decision. Calculating their speed, fuel, and the weather conditions, they determined they would try the longest flight in history. They would fly for 18 hours in the air before attempting a landing to refuel. It was dangerous, but a risk both men were willing to take. The conditions were difficult:

The weather began to grow thicker every minute as we tore across that sea in the darkest hours of the moonless night. By the time we were out over the middle of it…I was forced down to within a few feet of the water. A few bumps warned me that side gusts were hitting the wing. The gusts were so violent that I might have been flying through a mountain pass like some I had run across, which actually threw the ship momentarily out of control. But I knew there was nothing except water underneath. [8]

After a while, Wiley grew tired of flying just above the waves of the choppy sea and decided to increase his altitude, even though it meant he would be flying blind. He had practiced this ability in his preflight preparations. He relaxed, kept his eye on his instruments, and made his way through the dark skies. He

flew through hail, rain, mist, and drizzle, unable to see anything outside his window.

Every few hours Wiley would lift the *Winnie Mae* just above the clouds to allow Gatty to chart their location by getting a clear view of the stars and moon. Unfortunately, the maps that the Russians provided gave inaccurate readings regarding the heights of the peaks over which they were flying. Several times Wiley had to pull the *Winnie Mae* up into sharp climbs to avoid flying into the side of a mountain. Gatty shouted, "Say! That isn't on the map at all…Either these elevations are all wrong or our altimeter is haywire." Wiley did not have time to wonder, he had to get out of the way of the mountains. From then on he referred to it as the "maybe-it's-right-map." [9]

Gatty took a quick reading as they passed over St. Lawrence Island. He determined that they had only two hours of fuel left to get to Solomon Island. Then the fog closed in again.

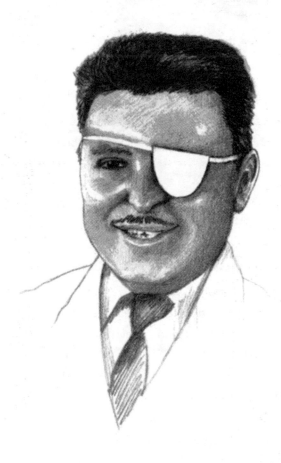

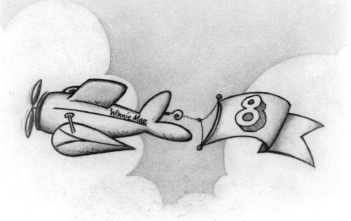

EIGHT DAYS

"It's all downhill from here…."
—Wiley Post

When Fort Davis and Solomon were in sight, the men knew they had accomplished an amazing feat. Wiley Post and Harold Gatty had together found their way over uncharted mountains and bodies of water, in "almost a full earth's day in a tiny airplane."

Once again, the *Winnie Mae* had come through for Wiley and he sat her down to rest on a sandy beach. When the ship stopped in the sand with her motor idling she throbbed "like a tired runner," her fuel tanks were almost on empty. [1]

It was early afternoon when they arrived to refuel at Solomon, a trading post and native village east of Nome. They planned to head to Fairbanks without delay.

The fuel tanks were topped off at 100 gallons. As Wiley taxied along the beach for take-off, suddenly the *Winnie Mae* started to sink into the sand. With a quick push, Wiley "banged the throttle open," hoping to pull her out of the quagmire. But it was too late. "With a loud slap," the propeller sliced into the sand and bent both tips on the blades. Fortunately, Wiley was able to cut the engine just in time to save the plane from "making an exhibition of herself by standing on her nose." Had that happened the trip would have been over. [2]

Here was where Wiley's mechanical training on farm equipment all those years ago paid off. He jumped out of the plane and used a wrench, a broken-handled hammer, and a round rock he found on the beach to straighten out the tips so "they would at least fan the air in the right direction." In five minutes the repairs were completed and they were ready for take-off. Gatty called out "all clear" and Wiley hit the switch.

Unfortunately, the engine backfired and the propeller flew out of Gatty's hands. Before he could get out of the way, one of the blades hit him in the shoulder above the heart almost breaking his ribs and knocking him to the ground. As he jumped away, the propeller came around again and hit him in the elbow, which momentarily paralyzed his left arm, leaving a bad bruise.

It was his luck that the flat side of the blade hit him, if the prop had been going the other way, "he might have been sliced in two." [3]

Although the pain was severe, Gatty quickly recovered, jumped into the back of the plane, and they were off. They made it to Fairbanks in less than four hours, where expert Pan Alaska Airways mechanics gladly went to work on the *Winnie Mae*. Not only did they "wipe her down, refuel, and oil her," but they also gave her a shiny new propeller. While the mechanics worked on the *Winnie Mae*, the fliers got some much-needed sleep at a nearby hotel.

Rested and excited to start the final 3,000 miles to New York, the men hardly spoke as they left Fairbanks and made their way to Canada. They were about to achieve a new world record:

Our trip was nearly over. Success was within our grasp. When we turned out the light…we both agreed that nothing short of fire, earthquake, or some other unforeseen catastrophe beyond [our] control…could stop us from setting a record, which should withstand the snipers and sharpshooters of aviation for some time to come. [4]

Gatty felt sure they were going to set a new aviation record, but the loneliness of the flight was frustrating him. He thought to himself, "Who cares? Is it worth this nerve-wracking dive through the rain, or putting my family through the worry I know they must be having? Good old Wiley! He just sits up there and flies." [5]

When they crossed over from the western to the eastern slope of the Rocky Mountains, Wiley shouted, "It's all downhill from here in, kid."

Gatty responded, "Give her all she can take and let's get this leg over." [6]

As Edmonton's muddy runway came into view, Wiley remarked, "Gee, I wish we had this crate mounted on floats." A huge crowd waited in the pouring rain as Wiley half skidded and half flew the airplane up the muddy runway directly to the front of the hangar. He was not about to stop short and get stuck in the mud again.

The excited crowd broke through the police lines and crowded around the plane. Wiley and Gatty stayed inside while the police attempted to restore order. When the fliers emerged from the cockpit a reporter stuck a microphone in front of Wiley, but all he could think to say was that, "he was tired of sitting down." [7]

After surveying the condition of the runway, Wiley was worried because he knew it would be days before it was dry enough to take off again. Gatty had so much confidence in Wiley by this time that he "…felt sure that, somehow or other Wiley and the *Winnie Mae* would manage to get off, even if we had to take an acre or two of wheat soil with us." [8]

The fliers were exhausted and concerned, but a Canadian airmail pilot came to the rescue. He suggested that Portage Avenue, a straight two-mile street that ran from the airport to downtown Edmonton, could be turned into a runway. Wiley inspected the street and agreed that it was a logical solution to the problem. The fliers were assured that everything would be ready for their take-off the next morning and, in the meantime, they could rest at the hotel.

Large crowds of people arrived again the next morning. During the night, electricians had carefully removed all of the electrical wires along both sides of the street and the street cleaners had swept the roadway to ensure that the plane could take off safely. The *Winnie Mae* was spotlessly clean as it waited at the end of Portage Avenue for its two famous fliers to come aboard.

Canadian mounted policemen cleared the traffic from the road. The rain had finally stopped as the *Winnie Mae* rushed along the narrow street. Curbs and electric light poles rushed so near the wing tips that Wiley was "just a little scared." By the time they reached the first turn in the street, they were 500 feet above the pavement. As Wiley flew over the Hotel MacDonald, where they had spent the night, the maitre d' was "out on the roof with his whole army of bellhops in array" to salute them going by. [9]

It was only a few hours later that the *Winnie Mae* entered the United States of America, just north of Bessemer Junction, Michigan.

It was July 1, 1931 and the flight of the *Winnie Mae* was the top news story around the world. Americans were gathered around their radios, as 5,000 people greeted Wiley and Gatty at a final fuel stop at the Municipal Airport in Cleveland, Ohio. Wiley said later that he "…was getting used to being mobbed by this time, but Gatty was developing a desire for seclusion. He would duck as soon as a group started toward us, and someone would have to drag him back." [10]

When reporters interviewed the fliers, they had little to say, as usual. Gatty told his wife and children that he could not wait to see them and he discussed the differences, as he saw them, between himself and Wiley. "We have a little trouble understand-ing each other. The trouble is I speak English and Wiley speaks Oklahoman." [11]

When the *Winnie Mae* took off from Cleveland, there was only one final destination for these adventurers, New York City. Be-cause they were flying a familiar airmail route, they relaxed and prepared for their big arrival. The sight of New York City excited Wiley:

Then came the biggest thrill of my life and of Harold's too,
for that matter, the New York sky line. What a sight! We had
gone all the way around the world for a glimpse of it from
the west! [12]

When they arrived at Roosevelt Field, Wiley proudly flew in over the hangars and delighted the enormous crowd by making an extra turn around the airport. He sat the *Winnie Mae* down on the runway and yelled back at Gatty, "Well, here we are, kid." [13]

Walter Ward, the official timekeeper of the National Aeronautic Association, announced the record time, eight days, 15 hours, 51 minutes. The "two young men in a hurry," as one newspaper called them, had flown 15,474 miles with an actual flight time of only 107 hours and two minutes. It was by far a new world record for air travel. They had averaged a phenomenal 146 miles an hour. No man had ever flown faster or farther in a single flight. "Gee," said Gatty, "let them shoot a while at that!" He knew it would be a long time before anybody broke the record they had just set. [14]

Through hard work and determination, Wiley Post and Harold Gatty had successfully turned their dream into a reality...in only eight days.

Around the world, huge crowds surrounded Wiley and the Winnie Mae. *Courtesy of* The Daily Oklahoman.

HOME AGAIN

"I knew they would do it."
—Mae Post

The large crowds at Roosevelt Field in New York were cheering wildly as the *Winnie Mae* made its way down the runway. Nearly 10,000 people climbed over fences and broke through police lines to get close to the airplane. Later, a *New York Times* reporter said of the scene, "They had flown around the world in less than nine days…and the crowds that cheered them seemed to feel that nothing but the arrival of men from Mars could dim the wonder of it." [1]

Both aviators were very tired and their faces showed it, as they only had 15 hours of sleep in the previous eight days. Two policemen escorted Mae Post out to the plane where she greeted Wiley with tears in her eyes. Throughout the long wait, she had remained confident. When Wiley began an air adventure his family accepted it as virtually already accomplished. Knowing his skill and determination, they had supreme confidence in his ability. His parents spent the entire course of his flight calmly working on their farm near Maysville. Because they had no telephone, their son Arthur occasionally delivered news of the flight.

Exhausted, Gatty pulled himself from the plane and sat on the wing. Wiley simply greeted his fans and said, "Well, we had a good time." As usual, he was not much of a speaker, just a superb pilot. In three short years Wiley had gone from being an unknown barnstormer to the world's most famous pilot. [2]

President Herbert Hoover welcomed the two fliers during a visit to the White House and there were numerous celebrations all over the country. Wiley later said, "All I know of the next few days is a muddle. The rest I planned never came. We were wined and dined until the very sight of food made me shudder." [3]

Reporters from every news service and every local, state, and national newspaper wanted to interview the two new celebrities. Wiley must have thought flying around the world was easier than all the commitments he had to honor on his return. The *New York Times* had followed the entire flight with daily stories and editorials that praised the accomplishments of the two young pilots, calling it "a test of men, fabric, and engine." [4]

The Daily Oklahoman suggested that Wiley's flight had accomplished his mission of giving Americans confidence in the safety of air travel and predicted what today has become ordinary:

Such feats as that of Post and Gatty are destined to become commonplace before the world is very much older. Ere long, the world will pay no more attention to the feat cheered so insanely at Roosevelt Field Wednesday than it will to a morning flight from New York to Philadelphia. The future of the human race is in the air. [5]

World leaders praised the accomplishments of Wiley and

Gatty and foreign newspapers proclaimed the success of the trip. The aviators had indeed accomplished the unimaginable. They were given a hero's welcome along Broadway in New York City with the city's largest ticker-tape parade, surpassing even the one for Lindbergh's flight.

When the fliers were introduced at a New York reception given in their honor, the plane that had carried them around the world also was given her due, "It left Roosevelt Field as the *Winnie Mae*…over Russia and the Far North you decided that it was the *Winnie Must*. And when you returned to Roosevelt Field it became the *Winnie Did*."

Wiley timidly thanked the people of New York and its mayor for the great celebration; it was his first public speech. A friend later observed, "All Wiley knows how to do is to fly. He doesn't know how to talk. A flier like Wiley can't be bothered to talk." [6]

Later, Wiley wrote a story that was especially created for the *New York Times* July 3 edition where he was able to more clearly summarize his hopes and dreams for the impact of the flight on the field of aviation:

> *We have great hopes that we may have helped bring the time closer when commercial aviation will span the seas and the land, and bring all peoples closer together…One thing I learned is that a man can sit in a plane, stay there for hours, be perfectly safe and get where he is going to even if he can't see anything beyond the instrument board. We did that repeatedly in this flight, and I would think that the general public's just knowing that such a thing was possible would increase confidence in aviation.* [7]

After returning home, Wiley had some difficulty in adjusting to the lack of sleep he had experienced on the long flight. He yawned frequently and failed to respond to questions from reporters. Gatty relayed them on to him, and he said, "I'm still pretty deaf, but I'll be able to hear pretty well by tomorrow. As a matter of fact, I could hear better in the plane than I could on land, and it is the absence of the motor's vibration that makes it hard for me to hear now." [8]

After all was said and done regarding the ability of the pilots, the aviation community was even more amazed at the mechanical and technical success of the mission. Other than the four sparkplugs that Wiley replaced, and very little servicing that the engine required, the *Winnie Mae* never sputtered. The fliers took no spare parts and made no significant repairs on the entire trip.

Oklahomans, as well as all Americans, were proud of Wiley for his history-making flight. The nation was suffering in the Great Depression and the amazing adventure of Wiley and Gatty gave people hope and an escape from the troubles of the day.

The budding field of aeronautics had many strong advocates including native Oklahoman Will Rogers. An early supporter of aviation, Rogers was one of the most popular entertainers and humorists of the day. His humor was balanced and good natured, though critical of contemporary affairs and political figures. Rogers realized early on that aviation was the future of travel and he took every chance he could to fly. By 1933, he had been a passenger on so many flights and promoted flying so extensively that he was named "the patron saint of aviation."

Rogers was the most widely read newspaper columnist in the

world and he often mentioned the adventures of the aviation pioneers of the era and informed his readers of flight records as they were set and broken. While they were on the around-the-world flight, Rogers told the nation:

> *No news today as big as this Post and Gatty, that are making this world of ours like the size of a watermelon. This pilot Post is an old one-eyed Oklahoma boy. He has just got the good eye glued on the horizon and he is going to find that horizon if it meets the earth anywhere, and…this Gatty, just give him a compass and one peek at the Giant Dipper and he can tell you where you are even if you ain't there. This is one ship I would have loved to been a stowaway on.* [9]

Rogers first met Wiley after the 1931 around-the-world flight and they became friends. When he wrote a special column about F.C. Hall's willingness to pay for the record-breaking flight, Hall wrote Rogers back informing him that Rogers's own hometown of Claremore, Oklahoma was throwing a reception for the fliers and invited him to come. Rogers suspected that Wiley and Gatty probably would not go unless they could fly in, and he knew that the town had no airport. So, "the old town [Claremore] got busy and in five days built the dandiest little airport you ever saw."

After the flight, F.C. Hall agreed to sell the *Winnie Mae* to Wiley for $21,200. Wiley gave Rogers his first ride in the record-setting plane, flying him to the banquet at Claremore. Rogers introduced the fliers to the audience on July 2, 1931 at the opening of the new airport by saying:

> *We are gathered here at these bountiful tables to do honor to two gentlemen who knew that the world was cockeyed, but wasn't right sure it was round…*
>
> *The physical hardship of this trip will stand out above all others. These birds stayed awake over seven full days out of eight, in fact they haven't had any sleep yet. There must be no worse torture and misery in the world than to have to keep going, when it looks and feels like you can't possibly hold your eyes open, and how wide theirs had to be open? That's what you call a sustained effort…They carried no parachutes, or rubber life boats, they simply made it or else…*
>
> *Mr. Post the pilot is another Oklahoman…He got his mechanical knowledge from working in a garage…He had*

*no ambition about going around the world but he could
take a wrench and go round the bolts on a Ford rim in record
time…That's why away up in Siberia when the ship hit in the
mud and tipped over on her nose, and did enough damage
to have sent most pilots back on the train, why he just took
a hammer and some barbed wire and fixed it so it added ten
miles more an hour. The old garage training came in handy.*

*He piloted the plane on the whole trip. He was raised
on a Texas "norther" and weaned on an Oklahoma "cyclone,"
so a little fog looked like a clear day to him…He is a determined looking little rascal, and when he says quit, you can be
sure there will be no more gas, or no more air…* [10]

In November, Wiley appeared in Chicago and was obviously
unhappy about his future in aviation. While the outside world
only saw a famous flier who had traveled around the earth in
record time, Wiley told a newspaper reporter that his trip around
the world meant nothing for aviation and that it would be
impossible to make any money as a pilot. For the remainder of
his short life, Wiley often wanted to be left completely alone. It
seemed the depression that had plagued him during his stint in
prison had returned.

Wiley never stopped dreaming, however, and less than a
month later, he announced that he would attempt a non-stop
flight from Tokyo to Seattle. No one had, as yet, flown non-stop
across the Pacific and Wiley wanted to be the first to do it. Two
months later, however, two pilots made a successful trans-Pacific
flight from Japan to Wenatchee, Washington. Wiley decided
to call off his flight because, "Wiley Post always tried to do new

things, and in new ways, that would leave a historic milestone
along the path of progress of manned flight…it was not his way
to fly in the tracks of other men, simply for the sake of setting
a new record." If he could not be first at something, he would
move on to the next challenge. [11]

Wiley began looking for a new way to fund another trip
around the world. At the same time, The Smithsonian Institution
in Washington, D.C. offered to buy the *Winnie Mae* if Wiley could
get people to contribute to its purchase. However, he was not
about to sell his beloved record-breaking airplane just yet. For
the world was about to witness Wiley Post's next dream come
true, flying around the world completely alone.

On July 2, 1931, Wiley Post and Harold Gatty were honored with a ticker-tape parade in
New York City. *Courtesy of Oklahoma Historical Society.*

SOLO

"See you in six days or else…"
—Wiley Post

In 1932, Wiley longed to fly alone around the world. He would not need a navigator this time because he would be using new instruments that had been developed to take over much of the work of holding a set course.

That summer, fliers Jimmy Mattern and Bennett Griffin tried to break the eight-day around-the-world record of the *Winnie Mae*. They followed the same route of Wiley and Gatty, but crash landed in Russia. The record remained unbroken! [1]

Unsuccessful in their team effort to beat his record, Mattern and Griffin heard that Wiley was planning to fly around the world alone and quickly made plans to try to beat him to it. They flipped a coin to see who would pilot the plane. Mattern won and prepared for the flight.

Wiley spent the next year making improvements to his plane. His first concern was that the *Winnie Mae*, made primarily out of plywood, was becoming outdated and the newer twin-engine, all-metal aircrafts were becoming popular. However, Wiley knew he could not afford a new airplane, so he began preparing the *Winnie Mae* for the task ahead.

In March of 1933, Wiley installed a Sperry automatic pilot to assist him in flying alone around the globe. He called the instrument, "Mechanical Mike." The device weighed 70 pounds and Wiley was allowed to mount the autopilot in his plane on the condition that he would not carry any passengers. [2]

Wiley tested the new autopilot in late March on a trip from Oklahoma City to Mexico. The system worked well and allowed Wiley to fly long distances during the trip without always having to man the controls. He wanted another opinion about its effectiveness so he asked his good friend and experienced pilot, Luther "Red" Gray, to verify his findings by taking a short flight with him. It almost cost them their lives.

The day of the flight, Gray noticed that the fuel gauge indicated "empty," but Wiley persuaded Gray to take off because he had refueled the plane the night before and was sure there was enough gas for the short test flight. What Wiley did not know was that teenagers had slipped into the airport the night before and drained all of the plane's gas for their cars. He assured Gray that the gauge must be wrong, gunned the engine and headed down the turf runway. The plane reached an altitude of about 50 feet when the engine quit. The fuel tanks were empty! Gray brought the *Winnie Mae* back to earth before crashing into a peach orchard at the end of the field.

Gray's experience in flying for Braniff Airways apparently saved the *Winnie Mae* from complete destruction. The fuselage of the plane split open and the propeller and engine were damaged, but Wiley was able to get her repaired. He was $600 short of being able to pay for the repairs, but several friends donated their off-hours to work on the famous plane. Wiley was so grateful for their help that he later saw that each man was paid double for his work. [3]

With a repaired and reconditioned plane, Wiley had large fuel tanks installed in the cabin, raising the fuel capacity to 645 gallons. The extra fuel would allow him to make fewer stops, saving him valuable time.

Wiley announced his solo flight plan in an interview with the *New York Times*. He would fly nonstop from New York to Berlin, almost 4,000 miles, an incredible distance to travel without refueling. Wiley planned only five refueling stops compared with 14 stops on his 1931 around-the-world flight. He was confident he could beat his old record and prove that he could both pilot and navigate on a world-record flight.

Outfitting a plane for a long-distance flight was an expensive undertaking and the need for financial support always was a problem. Wiley no longer had F.C. Hall to back his ventures and he needed someone to assist in financing the flight. Harry G. Frederickson, a wealthy Oklahoma City businessman, made a deal to raise the money needed for the venture for ten percent of the profits. Wiley made one condition that all contributions to the flight should come from Oklahomans interested in aviation.

Everyone from Stanley Draper and oilman Frank Phillips to Oklahoma Natural Gas and John A. Brown agreed to fund Wiley's newest adventure and $40,000 was raised for the historic flight. Wiley also convinced many of the country's leading aircraft manufacturers to donate supplies.

The around-the-world flight would be the ultimate test for the Sperry Robot Pilot, which was of special interest to the United States Army. Another device that needed to be tested on behalf of the U.S. Army Signal Corps was the "radio compass," or Automatic Direction Finder (ADF), which allowed pilots to be completely independent of any ground signaling system. The device would be attached to the outside of a plane and radio signals would hopefully allow pilots to stay on a predetermined course, regardless of wind and visibility conditions.

It was clear that navigating a plane was a lot less complicated than it had been in 1931, but most of the new devices needed a significant test to prove their airworthiness. Wiley intended to give them the ultimate test. The *New York Times* reported that,

"He [Post] will ride around the world on radio waves while the robot flies the plane." [4]

One of the improvements added to the plane was a "rather ingenious device" Wiley could use to grease the rocker boxes in the engine during flight. This tool would reduce the likelihood of an emergency and minimize the need for extensive ground maintenance. [5]

Wiley used the same training methods to prepare for his new adventure that he had employed before the 1931 flight. He limited his intake of food and broke his regular sleeping habits. He took long walks and studied maps, memorizing names and distances. He often spent all night at the airport, sitting alone in the cockpit of the *Winnie Mae* with his eye open. He had done all this before, but it was no less demanding the second time around. [6]

Wiley was disappointed when he first heard that Jimmy Mattern already had begun a solo flight around the world in June of 1933. Mattern took off from New York in his airplane called *Century of Progress*. Though the two pilots were friendly rivals, Wiley made it clear that he would not be rushed. He had made a decision that he would not begin his flight until his plane was ready and the weather was ideal. He went on about his business of preparing the *Winnie Mae*.

Mattern made it to Norway, where he refueled and flew on to Moscow. Ten days later, Mattern took off from Kharbarovsk in Siberia for Nome, Alaska, but never made it to his destination.

For two weeks the world waited to hear from Mattern, then news came that he was alive. His engine had stalled over the

Siberian tundra and he was forced to make a crash landing near the Anadyr River. He built a raft and floated downriver until he was rescued by a group of Eskimos. Wiley now knew that he alone had the opportunity to be the first pilot to fly solo around the world.

Wiley's goal was to leave New York as close to July 1 as possible. With that date in mind, he left Oklahoma City. With dozens of changes and repairs to his plane, Wiley felt the *Winnie Mae* was ready to take on the world. [7]

After arriving at Floyd Bennett Field, now John F. Kennedy International Airport, some unusual and frightening things began to happen. Someone tried to damage the plane's engine and Wiley started receiving threatening letters. The City of New York immediately assigned police to guard Wiley and Mae. Soldiers also were guarding the *Winnie Mae*, because the ADF that had

Wiley stands with aviation hero Charles Lindbergh, center, and Bennett Griffin, the pilot who joined Jimmy Mattern in July of 1932 in the hopes of shattering Post and Gatty's original around-the-world record. *Courtesy of Oklahoma Historical Society.*

been installed was considered government property and was still top-secret.

Wiley waited as squalls and cold fronts appeared over the Atlantic Ocean, keeping him grounded for four weeks. This time Wiley was less impatient. He and Mae tried to do some sight-seeing in the city. "He could move around New York unrecognized by inserting his glass eye instead of wearing his famous white eye patch." Finally, on July 15, Wiley decided it was time to go. [8]

For this flight, Wiley wore the white patch over his eye, a change from the 1931 flight where he had used his glass eye, which became so cold over Siberia and Alaska that it had caused him relentless headaches.

Wiley told Mae, "See you in six days or else." The *Winnie Mae* sat quietly, ready to carry its pilot into one of the greatest episodes in history.

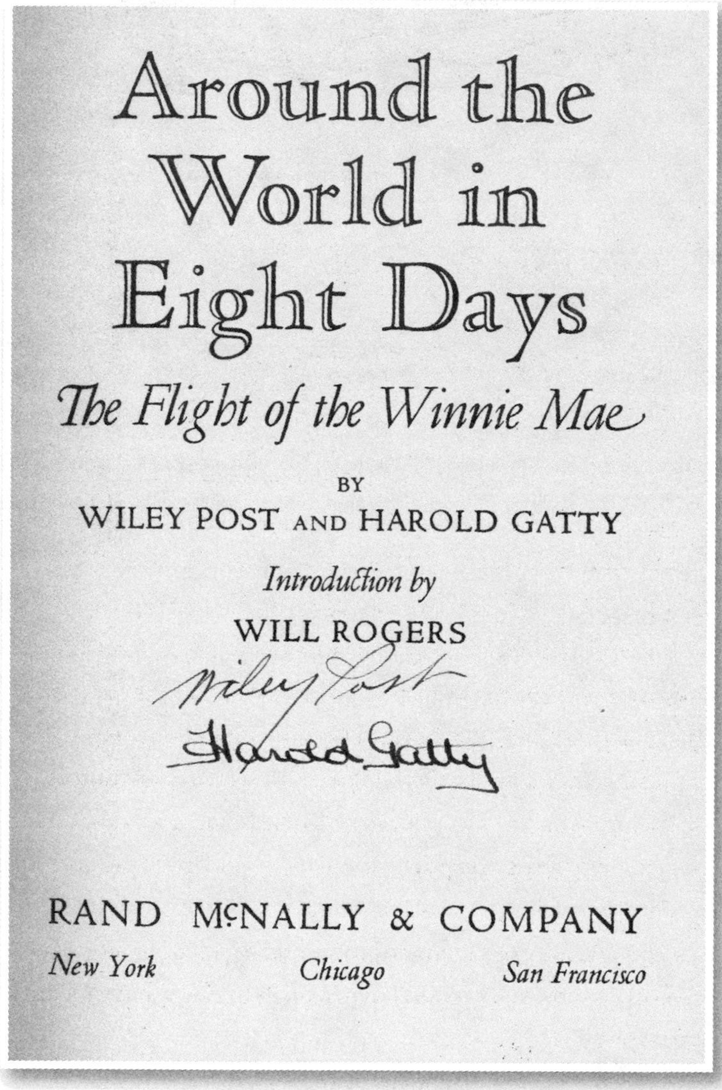

Around the World in Eight Days

The Flight of the Winnie Mae

BY

WILEY POST AND HAROLD GATTY

Introduction by

WILL ROGERS

Wiley Post

Harold Gatty

RAND McNALLY & COMPANY

New York   *Chicago*   *San Francisco*

A first edition cover of Post and Gatty's book, *Around the World in Eight Days*, autographed by the authors.

AROUND THE WORLD . . . ALONE

"He is a one-eyed Superman."
–Newspaper Reporters in 1933

At 5:10 a.m. on July 15, 1933, Wiley sent the *Winnie Mae* charging down the runway. Wiley's take-off "sent tingles up the spines of even the hardened onlookers." Mae and friend, Red Gray, followed him in another airplane for the first few miles until he "disappeared into the fog." Because of the heavy load of fuel, Mae was concerned that he might not make it off the runway. "That plane really trembled from the load, but he made it." [1]

The Sperry autopilot worked perfectly as Wiley encountered a thick fog bank just five minutes into the flight. Flying blind for the next two hours, the "Mechanical Mike" took over the controls.

Will Rogers wrote in his July 16 column, "I will bet you that this Wiley Post makes it around the world and breaks his own record. I would have liked to have been in there with Post instead of the robot."

The radio signals picked up by the ADF in the *Winnie Mae* were especially helpful to Wiley. His first flight with Gatty had been lonely, with hardly any radio contact, but this time he picked up radio stations providing special broadcasts just for him.

When Wiley landed in Berlin, a large crowd was assembled for his arrival and Germany's new Chancellor, Adolf Hitler, greeted the famous aviator. The *Winnie Mae* had flown 3,942 miles at an average of 153.5 miles per hour, shattering the previous trans-Atlantic records of Charles Lindbergh and Clarence Chamberlin. A *New York Times* reporter described Wiley's condition when he greeted the large crowds, "Post plainly showed the effects of his flight across the ocean. His dark gray suit was spic and span, but his face was drawn and his one good eye was bloodshot." [2]

Though he did not sleep at all on the flight to Berlin, Wiley felt he was in good enough condition to continue on to Novosibirsk. He was proud of the way his plane had performed, saying "…even the mechanics [at Berlin] marveled at her fit condition after my hard drive across the Atlantic. Not a single gadget was out of order." [3]

When Wiley took off for Russia, he immediately began experiencing problems with the Sperry autopilot and realized that several of his maps were missing. He decided to press on and stopped at Koenigsberg to have the autopilot repaired and to obtain medical attention. His eye socket was irritated and inflamed, so when he landed he found a local doctor who treated it with boric acid. Because the mechanics at Koenigsberg had no means to diagnose or fix the problems with the autopilot, he decided to sleep for six hours before continuing the flight to Moscow for repairs.

In his hurry to leave for Moscow, he forgot his suitcase with all his personal belongings. He would have to remain in the clothes he was wearing for the rest of the trip, but his wardrobe was the least of his worries. He was behind schedule and eager to make up lost time.

When Wiley arrived in Moscow, three doctors examined him and found him to be in excellent condition, showing no signs of fatigue. One of the Russian doctors said that he had never met a pilot with such "steady, solid nerves and such a regular pulse" after such an exhausting flight. [4]

While mechanics repaired oil lines to the autopilot, Wiley got a haircut and shave and told a *New York Times* reporter that he was not tired and that "...any American pioneer could do without sleep for a week." [5]

At 5:10 p.m. word came from the Russian mechanics that the plane was ready to go. Wiley wasted no more time. The 13-hour-and-15-minute flight from Moscow to Novosibirsk was one of the most difficult of Wiley's career. He almost scraped the top of a hill as he flew through fog and rain and had to find his way through a mountain pass. Wiley later said if there had been a parachute on the *Winnie Mae*, he would have jumped out rather than risk the flight through those mountains. For brief periods, he climbed to 21,000 feet to get above the bad weather. Wiley knew how long he could endure the lack of proper oxygen at high altitudes, and always brought the *Winnie Mae* back to a lower altitude before the lack of oxygen could hurt him.

Though he had been cautious, Wiley became a bit disoriented on his way to Novosibirsk. The cold air made him drowsy and his oxygen-deprived lungs ached. He sat the *Winnie Mae* down near a mountain road to try to find out where he was. He tried to communicate with two peasants who had come along, but had to finally use sign language. One peasant said Novosibirsk was 300 miles to the west; the other said the town was 1,500 miles to the east. Confused, Wiley took off and guessed correctly that he was still west of Novosibirsk.

Fay Gillis, the daughter of an American engineer in Russia and the aviation reporter in the Soviet Union for the *New York Herald Tribune*, was waiting for Wiley at Novosibirsk. She made sure that the grass on the runway was cut short, that there was a room awaiting him, and that there were a variety of meals prepared for him. The maps that he had left in Berlin also were replaced. After dictating a report about the flight to Fay, which she forwarded to the *New York Times*, he was ready to leave. Fay also sent a cable to Mae Post at the Roosevelt Hotel in New York:

WILEY BEEN AND GONE. ONLY STAYED TWO HOURS AND
A HALF. HE'S IN HIGH SPIRITS DESPITE BAD LUCK WITH
WEATHER. EXPECTS TO BE IN NEW YORK IN THREE DAYS.
HAVE FUN. [6]

Unexpected repairs and poor weather conditions were slow-
ing down the pace of the flight. On his way to Khabarovsk, the
autopilot malfunctioned again and Wiley had to land at Irkutsk
for repairs. As he flew toward Khabarovsk, he followed the Trans-
Siberian Railroad at a speed of almost 200 miles an hour. Then,
darkness and rain forced him to make an unscheduled stop at
Rukhlovo.

Wiley's drinking water supply had not been replenished at his
last stop and he was suffering from dehydration when he landed
at Rukhlovo. He tried to explain to his Russian hosts that he was
thirsty and needed water, not the liquor they were offering. They
could not understand him or his gestures, so he had to settle
for a glass of tea. Wiley would not get a glass of water until he
arrived in Alaska.

When Wiley arrived in Khabarovsk, Jimmy Mattern, who was
still in Siberia after his unsuccessful solo attempt, helped prepare
the weather reports for Wiley's use during the next leg of his
flight.

Leaving Russia, Wiley piloted the *Winnie Mae* through
clouds, flying by instruments and autopilot, as he made the
3,100-mile trip to Fairbanks, Alaska. Flying blind, he traversed
through mountains, some as high as 15,000 feet and hidden in
heavy clouds. Unsure of the maps he was given, he often had
to increase his altitude to avoid the peaks, depriving himself of
oxygen.

As mountains began to appear above the clouds, Wiley crossed the Bering Strait and was above Alaska. Visibility was poor as he reached the coast and he became disoriented. Unable to pick up radio signals from Fairbanks, he was lost over central Alaska. What he did not know at the time was that his ADF system, which was so vital to his navigation, had completely stopped working. He could not see the ground nor could he contact anyone on the ground.

For seven hours he dodged mountains and followed rivers before landing at an airport in the small mining town of Flat. He was 31 hours ahead of his 1931 record and needed to rest.

The makeshift runway at Flat's airport was little more than 700 feet long and the *Winnie Mae* rolled down the short, grassy field. It was then that Wiley spied a ditch! He was unable to stop in time and the she skidded into the gully. She fell over on her right wing, and the right leg of her landing gear crumpled. Her tail came up and her nose drove into the ground, bending the propeller. [7]

Wiley made his way to a telephone and called Joe Crosson, a good friend and chief pilot for Pan Alaska Airways in Fairbanks. Crosson and three other mechanics soon arrived with a new propeller and landing gear for the *Winnie Mae*.

Early the next morning Wiley followed Crosson's plane to Fairbanks for refueling and repair of the ADF. After an eight-hour delay caused by bad weather in Canada, Wiley began a stressful nine-hour flight to Edmonton, Alberta. He was flying at 21,000 feet over the mountains, with air temperatures dipping to six degrees below zero. He later said that this period was the most frightening of the whole trip:

Ice was forming on my ship and forcing me down at the rate
of 100 feet a minute. I had the motor wide open, but I could
not get an air speed above 125 miles and I kept going down.
I knew the mountains came up to 15,000 feet there, and if
I ever had got down to 16,000 I would be gone. I kept figur-
ing every minute I had better fasten my parachute. [8]

After he took off from Edmonton, Wiley was so tired he let
the autopilot do the flying while he tried to rest. In order to
remain as alert as possible, he tied a wrench to his finger with a
piece of string. He held the wrench in his hand and whenever
he slipped into too deep a sleep, his hand would relax and the
wrench would fall, jerk his finger, and wake him up. Wiley later
said, "I'll bet I fell asleep two hundred times before I reached New
York City." [9]

Signals from radio stations broadcasting all across America
allowed him to use his ADF to fly a perfect course all the way
home. Wiley heard live radio broadcasts from New York City es-
timating his time of arrival. This leg of the trip was probably the

most enjoyable for Wiley, and surely the most exciting. Not only was he the first man to fly around the world twice, but he was the first man to do it all alone. And, he was almost home.

Fifty thousand people were waiting for Wiley at Floyd Bennett Field in New York City on the evening of July 22, 1933. For the next few days, the entire world would celebrate Wiley's heroic efforts and shower him with genuine appreciation for his accomplishments.

Newspaper reporters described him as a "one-eyed superman," who could fly an airplane as if he had mystical powers. Mae Post, who lost about as much sleep as Wiley did on the flight, was ready for her husband to come home. The *New York Times* reported:

> In her smart blue ensemble she tripped through the corridor
> of the hotel and started for the flying field. She did not know
> it, but a brand new automobile was awaiting her there, a
> coupe her husband had purchased before starting on his
> flight and which he had arranged to present to her as a sur-
> prise on his return. She was to drive him away from the field
> in the new car after his landing. [10]

Just before midnight, the *Winnie Mae* could be heard making her descent back to earth and her lights gradually lit the night sky above the runway. As they touched down, Wiley and the *Winnie Mae* were "…engulfed by a swarm of humanity." [11]

Wiley peered out over the hatch, but it was some time before he could leave the plane. His clothes looked as if he had slept in them because he had. His trademark white eye patch, which Mae had sewn, was dirty so he borrowed a handkerchief to tie around his head and cover his eye socket.

Reporters asked Wiley about his experience and he said that he felt fine except for a terrible headache from the high altitudes. He admitted he was "not as tired as when Gatty and I did this thing two years ago" and summed up the trip by saying, "I have tried to make this flight with the idea of not killing myself, not only because I did not want to get killed, but because it would look bad for aviation."

Despite some major mishaps and making only 11 stops, Wiley had broken his 1931 around-the-world record by more than 21 hours. He made the trip in seven days, 18 hours, and 49 ½ minutes, with a total flying time of 115 hours and 36 ½ minutes.

Following the trip, doctors found that Wiley had shed eight pounds and slept less than one day out of the week. After a brief rest at the hotel, he returned to see if his *Winnie Mae* was okay and to remove some personal belongings from the plane. Then, the celebrations began.

Wiley's second big city parade was even larger than the first. Wiley rode along Broadway as ticker tape and tiny parachutes floated down on him. Thousands cheered his name. The next day Wiley and Mae took a train to Washington, D.C. to meet President Franklin D. Roosevelt.

Wiley had accomplished exactly what he set out to do. In the back of his mind he already had realized what his next mission would have to be. For it was on this journey that Wiley Post discovered something totally unexpected. The strong rivers of air at high altitudes that he had encountered on both his around-the-world flights remained an unproven myth to everyone but him.

Wiley Post and his beloved *Winnie Mae,* 1933. *Courtesy of Oklahoma Historical Society.*

NEW DISCOVERIES
AND EXCITING INVENTIONS

"That's the way I want to go, doing the things I want to do."
—Wiley Post

Wiley's solo flight had set aviation records. In addition, the two electronic devices he used for navigation—the Automatic Direction Finder and the Sperry Autopilot—saved him work. It also was clear that his record flight had ushered in a new era in aviation. Long-distance flying was no longer wishful thinking; it was now a reality thanks to Wiley.

Wiley would realize more profit from his solo flight than the one he took with Gatty, but he was disappointed to find that there was no demand for his services from private industry. He had unparalleled aviation experience and yet nobody asked his opinion or called upon his expertise.

Anyone listening carefully would have heard Wiley announce his next project only three days after returning from his record setting solo flight. Speaking before the Aeronautical Chamber of Commerce, he told guests that he planned to begin studies on high-altitude flying.

At the beginning of his lecture tour following the flight, Wiley spoke of new possibilities on the horizon for the airline industry. He predicted that regular flights across the ocean would soon be a common thing. He was right!

As the tour ended, Wiley turned his attention to testing the "thin air" called the stratosphere. Wiley Post prepared himself to explore something that few believed in or had ever experienced.

On his solo trip across Siberia, he reached heights above 20,000 feet, usually to avoid bad weather, but also to confirm the existence of the strong tail winds he had experienced on his first flight with Gatty. Because no other aviator had flown anywhere near that altitude without oxygen, no one else had discovered Wiley's "swift river of air." Little did Wiley know that this discovery would today stand as his greatest contribution to the advancement of aviation. [1]

Wiley was excited about high altitude flying in the stratosphere, the layer of the earth's atmosphere that is characterized by thin air, excellent visibility, superb weather conditions, and rapid currents of air that Wiley initially called "high winds."

There were two problems he had to confront at high altitudes—extremely low temperatures and lack of oxygen. Wiley knew that the *Winnie Mae*, built mostly out of plywood and wire, could not be pressurized to safely allow him enough oxygen to breathe so he had to come up with another plan.

Wiley reasoned that his body would have to be enclosed in some type of suit that would provide an oxygen-rich environment. He began working on a revolutionary idea to design and build a pressurized suit. If it was able to provide the needed oxygen to the pilot, as well as the oxygen-rich air that the motor would require, he saw no reason why a plane could not exceed 250 miles per hour in the "thin air" high above the earth. Wiley designed oxygen supply systems the *Winnie Mae* would require for high altitude flight; and, once again, she was significantly redesigned to accommodate his alterations. [2]

Late in 1933, Wiley began designing a personal pressurized outfit of clothing. He had drawings drafted of the pattern he had in mind and completed the paperwork for a patent on the revolutionary design. What Wiley designed ultimately became a prototype for the space suits that astronauts wear in space today.

Borrowing on the concept of deep-sea diving suits, Wiley called his friends at the B.F. Goodrich rubber plant in Los Angeles, California and asked them to build the suit so that oxygen could be piped into it from tanks of liquid oxygen. The engineers used Wiley's body measurements, then cut out patterns and designed a two-piece suit with an airtight belt. They attached pigskin gloves and rubber boots. The headgear was an aluminum helmet with a tiny window, bulges over the ears for headphones, and a small trap door over the mouth so he could eat and drink. The basic design of Wiley's first pressure suit was good, but it could not withstand atmospheric pressures and the suit split apart during a test.

Wiley decided to keep the helmet but redesign the rest of the suit. Unfortunately, he had gained almost 20 pounds since the original measurements were taken. When the second suit was constructed he was able to put it on, but could not take it off, and it had to be cut from his body and destroyed.

In August 1934, Wiley began testing a third and final pressure suit. It incorporated flexible elbow and knee sections and
had two separate layers. An inner rubber suit would conform to
Wiley's body, and an inflexible outer cloth suit would hold the
rubber suit in place. Before, Wiley had been measured while
lying on the ground, this time a metal outline of him sitting in a
"comfortable sitting position, as if he were in the cockpit" was
taken. Then the model was covered with liquid latex and the
molded form served as the inner layer of the suit. The outer layer
was reinforced and oxygen would enter the redesigned helmet
from the left side next to his missing eye. The helmet contained
earphones and a microphone. The new window could be left
open until the pilot reached an altitude that required oxygen,
then he could screw the window shut. [3]

Wiley took the world's first altitude-chamber test in a flight pressure suit at Wright Field on August 27, 1934. The suit tested well on two consecutive pressure tests and Wiley was ready for his test flight.

With the new suit, he flew the *Winnie Mae* to the Chicago World's Fair and attempted to set a world's altitude record. It would be the first public test of his invention. He reached an altitude of 40,000 feet and the pressure suit worked perfectly, making Wiley the first person in history to fly in a pressure suit using liquid oxygen at high altitudes. The world's first space suit was a success!

Wiley's third pressurized suit survived all of his high altitude attempts and is on display today at the Smithsonian's National Air & Space Museum in Washington, D.C. Sadly, the results of the Chicago flight could not be considered "official" because the attempt had to be supervised by representatives of the National Aeronautic Association.

Finding money to support his pressure suit experiments became difficult and Wiley needed a new sponsor. Frank Phillips, president of Phillips Petroleum, immediately agreed to fund Wiley's continuing experiments in stratospheric flights. His goal was to use Wiley's name and success to advertise his petroleum products. A deal was struck between Wiley and Phillips in which Wiley agreed to attempt to break the world altitude record in Bartlesville if Phillips would provide gasoline and oil.

Wiley moved his operations to Oklahoma again and flew the *Winnie Mae* to Phillips' headquarters in Bartlesville. He was now ready to attack the altitude record of 47,352 feet held by Italian

Air Force pilot Renato Donati, who died less than 24 hours after setting the record. Donati had worn a special helmet over his head, but nothing to equalize the pressure on his body.

Frank Phillips insisted that Wiley sign a document releasing Phillips Petroleum Company from liability in case Wiley was injured or killed during his high altitude attempts. Wiley said, "Sure, I know it's dangerous. If I get 'popped off,' that's the way I want to go, doing the things I want to do." [4]

Wiley's first serious attempt to break the altitude record came on December 7, 1934. He put on his pressure suit and took off from the Phillips Airport in Bartlesville. He flew in the stratosphere for two hours. An oxygen valve eventually malfunctioned, forcing him to land in Muskogee, Oklahoma, 80 miles southeast of where the flight originated. Wiley did not know at the time why he landed 80 miles from where he took off. He had discovered the "jet stream." [5]

An official from the National Aeronautic Association (NAA) had installed two high-altitude barographs in the *Winnie Mae* before the flight. While one of them indicated that Wiley had reached his goal of 50,000 feet, the second one had frozen at 35,000 feet, so the altitude record could not be confirmed. Later Wiley would report:

The thermometer outside registered 70 degrees below zero, yet I was comfortable. The flying suit worked perfectly after I had fastened the faceplate of my helmet and turned on the (external) supercharger at 20,000 feet—As a result of this flight I am convinced that airplanes can travel at terrific speeds above 30,000 feet by getting into the prevailing wind channel.

It was one of at least eight flights Wiley made to 50,000 feet in the *Winnie Mae*. The cold temperatures peeled paint from the plane, but it was man's first view from ten miles up. Wiley still had doubters who considered his belief in the "high winds" to be nothing more than a fantasy. He realized that the only way to convince them was to make a flight that "defied any reasonable explanation."[6]

He decided a cross-country flight would provide the proof that high altitude wind currents could speed air travel in an environment that was free of the complications and dangers of bad weather. To verify his record for the NAA, he would need two timers and observers—a starter and observer in Burbank, California where he would take off, and two more in New York to record his arrival.

In exchange for financial assistance for his research into stratospheric flight, Wiley agreed to carry specially marked airmail across the country for a budding new airline, Trans World Airlines (TWA). He loaded up the *Winnie Mae* with 150 pounds of United States Mail on February 22, 1935. With his pressure suit on, he climbed into his plane and left Burbank headed for New York. The purpose of the trip was to streak across the continent at 375 miles per hour in the thin air of the stratosphere.

Just thirty minutes into the flight, the engine began to throw oil. Wiley was in a dangerous situation, he had 300 gallons of fuel on board and no way to dump it. He had to shut off his engine at 24,500 feet and guide the plane to the ground. He called on his years of flying experience and landed softly on Muroc Dry Lake in the Mojave Desert, just 57 miles into his flight.

The *Winnie Mae* rolled to within 300 yards of a lone automobile stranded in the desert. H.E. Mertz, who ran the Muroc general store, was having car trouble and his head was under the car's hood when Wiley landed. In his pressurized suit, it was difficult for Wiley to get out of the plane, much less walk. The suit was not designed for hiking, so Wiley was exhausted by the time he reached Mertz's car. Mertz almost died of fright when Wiley, still in his pressure suit, tapped him on the shoulder to ask for help in getting out of the helmet and suit.

The man's knees buckled and he almost fell over. He ran around to the back of his auto and peered at me. I had a time calming him down but I finally succeeded and he helped me out of my oxygen helmet. "Gosh fellow," he exclaimed when he found his voice, "I was frightened stiff. I thought you had dropped out of the moon, or somewhere." [7]

Undeterred, Wiley continued to pursue his high-altitude flights. On March 5, 1935, he was making a flight from Burbank, California when he ran out of oxygen and had to make an emergency landing near Cleveland, Ohio. The statistics of the flight were historic, he had flown 2,035 miles in the record time of seven hours and 19 minutes, an average ground speed of 279 miles per hour. Wiley was now the first person to "ride" the jet stream.

Aviation experts were finally taking Wiley and his stratospheric flights seriously, the *New York Times* declared the Burbank-to-Cleveland flight to be the "...most startling development in aviation since Lindbergh spanned the Atlantic." [8]

Wiley tried to establish the existence of the "high winds" in one final test with the *Winnie Mae*. He would try to prove to the last disbeliever that aviation's future lay in high-altitude flight by beginning a fourth transcontinental flight on June 15, 1935. Everything was going well until engine trouble forced Wiley to land "dead-stick" in Wichita, Kansas, 1,188 miles into the flight. The very next day he decided it was time to sell the *Winnie Mae*. His friend Will Rogers suggested to the nation that the plane deserved a final resting place in the Smithsonian Institution and asked readers to help Wiley buy a new airplane:

Wiley Post, just about king of them all, can't break records getting to New York in a six-year-old plane, no matter if he takes it up so high that he coasts in. That Winnie Mae...*has already done more than any plane in the World. Twice it has broken records clear around the world, broken altitude records. He has thrown off his wheels and has forced landings on his 'belly.' And she never breaks a thing. So when Wiley gets ready to put her into the Smithsonian we all want to give him a hand.* [9]

On June 24, 1935, preparations were made for the Smithsonian to purchase the *Winnie Mae* for $25,000. Wiley was sad as he parked the plane near the hangar at the Bartlesville airport for the last time. With the *Winnie Mae* soon to be a museum artifact, the press began to speculate on what Wiley might do next. One thing was certain—Wiley needed a vacation and was ready to join his old friend Will Rogers on a breath-taking trip....to Alaska.

Today, this amazingly detailed replica of the *Winnie Mae* hangs in the grand atrium of the new Oklahoma History Center in Oklahoma City. Among the other unique exhibits from Wiley's life, visitors will see a detailed reproduction of the pressurized helmet created by Wiley. *Photo by Eric Dabney.*

WILEY AND WILL

"Great trip…Don't worry."
—Will Rogers

In February 1935, Wiley bought a low-wing hybrid airplane made from the parts of two different airplanes. He had some of the *Winnie Mae's* instruments installed and painted it red with a silver stripe.

Because the public still was concerned about the hazards of ocean crossings, Wiley began to plan an overland route to Europe that would only involve a short, 50-mile crossing of the Bering Strait. After crossing the water, the route would continue across Alaska and Siberia. Passengers could be confident that, except for the short amount of time spent over the Strait, they would be flying over land. Wiley planned an exploratory trip to demonstrate the efficiency of his proposed route with the help of his friend, Fay Gillis. It was to be a secret and it was up to Wiley to raise the funds and furnish the plane. Though PAN-AM Airlines turned down his idea, they suggested that his friend Will Rogers might be willing to sponsor at least part of the exploratory trip.

Wiley had envisioned that the trip would be part research and part vacation. Because he would be flying over Alaska and Siberia, where ice turned into shallow lakes, wheels would be a problem. He knew that he would need to equip his plane with pontoons, long tubes with canoe-shaped noses that float. For at least a portion of the trip, he determined that he would need a solid wing with an undercarriage for wheels that could be exchanged for pontoons when he needed to land on water. After crossing Siberia, he would have the wheels reinstalled.

Wiley found a Lockheed Explorer wing from a plane that had been destroyed in a crash. There was nothing wrong with the Explorer wing, however it was not designed for his plane. Wiley wanted Lockheed to attach it, but they refused. "The ship…incorporated two entirely different engineering designs and was regarded therefore, more or less, as a freak." [1]

Not to be discouraged, Wiley simply took his plane to a terminal at Burbank, California and had the work done there. Although there would ultimately be six fuel tanks on the plane, Wiley would have only one fuel gauge that told him how much gas he had in a 30-gallon emergency tank attached under the pilot's seat.

The Wasp engine on Wiley's plane was very powerful and used a great deal of fuel both on takeoff and during flight. In flight, when all the other tanks were emptied, Wiley could tap the emergency tank that would allow him one hour to find a place to land before the last of the fuel ran out. Because of the fuel weight, the equipment carried on the flight, and the non-retractable landing gear below the fuselage the plane was "nose-heavy." [2]

Wiley's new plane had no name. He gave it a number and said that was all that was necessary, though he sometimes called it "Aurora Borealis." Rogers called it "Post Toasty," but others, less impressed with its combination of borrowed parts, referred to it as "Wiley's Orphan."

Disappointed by PAN-AM's rejection of his job proposal, Wiley had another problem with which to contend. Fay Gillis, whom he had counted on to be his co-pilot and translator, called to tell him she would not be making the flight with him. With no sponsor to pick up the expenses, no income, and no flight partner, Wiley was at a dead end. It was then that he remembered Will Rogers. [3]

Will Rogers was "itching" to go to Alaska. He wrote about his interest in his March 10 weekly article:

I have never been to that Alaska. I am crazy to go up there some time. They do a lot of flying up there. There is some crack aviators. Wiley Post went back up there this last summer to visit one of 'em that had helped him out, and they went hunting in a plane. [4]

The two men spoke and agreed that Rogers would sponsor the trip and pay all the bills. Wiley would provide the transportation to places that neither had ever visited.

Rogers needed the rest that the trip would provide and said, "Well, we got all the time we want. When we feel like flying we'll take a little hop. When we feel like sitting, we'll just sit and visit awhile." [5]

After the plane had been outfitted, Wiley and Mae, along with Rogers, took a trip to New Mexico, Arizona, and Utah to determine how the plane would perform. "Whenever Wiley saw a promising stream with a meadow nearby, he would set the plane down and give the local fish a chance to bite. Rogers, who did not fish, claimed to have looked at cattle." [6]

The pontoons that Wiley ordered still had not arrived when he and Rogers were ready begin their trip. He settled on another set, made for a much larger airplane. Wiley flew to Seattle to have the pontoons installed on his plane. When Rogers met Wiley in Seattle, he described the plane, "...Ship looks mighty pretty. It's a bright red with a few trimmings of White stripes. The pontoons are awful big looking things but Wiley says 'none too big.'" [7]

On August 6, 1935, Rogers wrote about their departure from Seattle, "Well they've 'bout got the gas in: Wiley is getting nervous. I am anxious to get going too. I think we are going to have a great trip, see lots of country that not too many have seen." Then the two men took off for their first stop in Juneau, Alaska.

In his newspaper column, Rogers described Wiley's ability as a pilot and their trip from Seattle to Juneau, "There is millions of channels and islands and bays and all look alike to me but this boy [Wiley] turns up the right alley all the time." It was raining when the men arrived at Juneau and Wiley's friend, Joe Crosson, was there to greet them. That night on a radio broadcast on KINY, Rogers explained how they planned to conduct their trip, "…I'm not up here on any commission. Wiley and I are like a couple of country boys in an old Ford—we don't know where we are going and we don't care." [8]

When the weather cleared, Wiley started the engine, heading north to Dawson City, in Canada's Yukon Territory. While there, a reporter from the *Dawson News* interviewed Rogers, and at one point he made clear how he felt about the risks of flying by saying, "No riding in any railway contraption for me. What if the thing jumped the track? I prefer an honorable death in a plane, or falling off a horse." [9]

Everywhere Wiley and Will went on their trip, crowds gathered, wanting autographs and asking about their plans. He would tell them, "Me and Wiley are just a couple of Oklahoma boys trying to get along."

One of the stops on their sightseeing tour, Barrow, Alaska, held Rogers' immediate interest because of stories he had heard about an old trader there who had been the chief operator of a trading post and whaling station for 50 years. Joe Crosson had been telling them about Charlie Brower, known as the "King of the Arctic," and Rogers wanted to meet him.

Point Barrow is 600 miles east of the Bering Strait and is the most northern point of the North American continent. In 1935, Barrow was home to nine Caucasians and about 500 natives and known for its difficult weather conditions. With an early winter approaching that season, it often was covered in heavy fog and drizzle with zero visibility.

On August 14, the weather was bad at Barrow, so Wiley and Rogers flew back to Fairbanks to stay all night with Joe Crosson. The next morning, while Rogers was walking around town, Wiley and Joe looked at houses. Wiley was impressed with Joe's gold mine and loved everything about Alaska. Thinking that he and

Mae might someday live in Fairbanks, Wiley found a little house on Cushman Street and immediately rented it. Then, he and Joe went to the Fairbanks airport, and planned a trip to Point Barrow to meet Charlie Brower.

Rogers sent his last telegram to daughter Mary that morning: GREAT TRIP. WISH YOU WERE ALONG...GOING TO POINT BARROW TODAY. FURTHEST POINT OF LAND ON WHOLE AMERICAN CONTINENT. LOTS OF LOVE. DON'T WORRY. DAD

The morning weather reports from Barrow on August 15 were still not good, but Wiley decided to take off, hoping the weather would improve. He promised Joe, who tried to talk him out of taking off, that he would call for an update on the weather in Barrow later in the afternoon.

They decided that there was not enough room for a take-off with full fuel tanks on the small lake at Fairbanks. Wiley decided to leave with partially filled tanks and fly to Harding Lake, about 50 miles away, and have the tanks filled there. With the larger lake as his runway, he should have no difficulty getting the heavy fuel-laden plane off the water. The weather at Fairbanks was perfect, but the weather report at Point Barrow could not have been worse.

There was no telephone at the Harding Lake dock, so Wiley never called Barrow for the latest weather. If he had called, Sergeant Stanley Morgan would have reported dense fog and no visibility. Wiley took off doing something pilots are routinely cautioned against, he "made his own weather" and simply hoped for the best.

After flying several hours from Harding Lake, Wiley was

completely lost. The entire coast around Barrow was covered
with a thick blanket of fog. Wiley circled the area for hours, but
could not see any landmarks to help establish his location. He
finally caught sight of a small Eskimo hunting camp beside a
tidal river that flowed into the Arctic Ocean. Through the fog
and drizzle, Wiley settled the plane in a lagoon and stopped as
close to the shore as possible. He and Rogers stepped out to
ask directions to Point Barrow. Clair Okpeaha and his family told
them that Barrow was just a few miles north across the tundra.

The men climbed back into their plane and Wiley taxied the
plane across the river. Then, something strange happened. "The
Okpeahas heard the explosion of a backfire, 'like the sound of a
shotgun'…and the engine stopped. For the merest fraction of a
second the red plane seemed to hang in midair…Then, being in
a turning motion, it began to somersault and tumbled side over
side downward. It hit the shallow water head on, the impact
shearing off the right wing and breaking the floats, and fell onto
its back…Almost all of the plane remained visible. It had fallen
into two or three feet of water." [10]

The impact of the crash forced the engine back through the
body of the plane, instantly killing its famous occupants. Later
examination showed that Wiley had switched off his engine
before the plane hit the water, "…the act of a wise pilot, one
who…thought…of this small margin of safety when faced by
death." [11]

Wiley's watch, later recovered from the wreckage, stopped at
8:18 p.m. It was August 15, 1935.

THE END

"Red airplane, she blew up…"
—Clair Okpeaha

Clair Okpeaha, the Eskimo seal hunter who had pointed the way to Barrow, saw the plane plunge through the thick fog into the shallow water of the lagoon. Lying on its back, the plane's fuselage was broken and one wing was ripped off. Okpeaha ran to the edge of the water and said, "Halloo! Halloo!" There was no answer. [1]

Following the shoreline, it took Okpeaha quite some time to run the 15 miles to the United States Department of Interior station directed by Sergeant Stanley Morgan at Point Barrow.

The natives gathered around Okpeaha as he gasped out in broken English, "Airplane fall—maybe two mans die near my camp." Sergeant Morgan asked Okpeaha how he knew there were two men in the crashed plane.

He replied, "Me talked with mans."

Morgan asked, "When, after they fell?" '

"No," answered Okpeaha, "before they fell, when they come down on water and ask me how go Barrow, where Barrow is, how far."

"Did they tell you their names?"

"No," replied Okpeaha, "Mans no tell names, but big mans, two mans, one sore eye with bandage on eye, he and other man then to inside plane, and man with sore eye start engine, and go up, maybe ten fathoms [60 ft.] and then engine spit, start, then stop, start some more little, then plane fall just so [indicating with his hands a bank, and a fall on right wing, and a nose dive in to water, with a complete somersault forwards, as he expressed it.]"

Asked as to whether or not he waded out to the plane after the crash, Okpeaha said, "No me stand on sand spit forty feet away and holler to mans, but no answer, and so me hurry quick to Barrow to tell peoples quick." [2]

As Okpeaha was excitedly telling Thomas Brower the circumstances of the crash, his loud voice drew other Eskimos from their homes. He said, "…airplane she blew up." [3]

Brower and Morgan immediately put together a rescue team including a local schoolteacher and several native men and boys. Okpeaha was dispatched to notify Charles Brower, the man Wiley and Rogers were coming to visit and the civil authority in town, about the crash. It was only when Okpeaha described the men in the plane as "…one man with rag on sore eye and big man with boots" that the team realized it could be Wiley and Rogers. Another of Brower's sons, David Brower, was sent out with a power boat towing an oomiak, a native skin-covered flat bottom fishing boat, to pick up what they hoped would be the injured fliers. In their haste to get to the site, the teams left behind Dr. Henry Greist, the local physician.

The rescue teams took nearly three hours fighting strong currents and trying to avoid large chunks of ice before reaching the crash site on the morning of August 16. The plane had landed in only a few feet of clear water and was resting on its back, with one wing torn off and a pontoon sticking skyward.

Some of the natives had arrived before the rescue boats, smashed a hole in the cabin of the plane, removed Roger's body, and wrapped it in one of the sleeping bags taken from the wreckage. They had carefully placed the body on the edge of the lagoon. They also had removed the luggage and piled it on the beach.

Everything in the plane was broken, except for small objects. "Some of the women began to salvage the papers, charts and personal effects scattered around the site." [4] Roger's typewriter, though twisted out of shape, still held an unfinished column in it. They also found "…the book that Will must have been reading just before the landing at the lagoon, for tucked inside it, as a bookmark, were Will's reading glasses, miraculously unbroken. Soggy from floating in the brackish water, these personal effects now lay in neat stacks on the shore." [5]

When the engine had been forced back into the cabin, it had pinned Wiley against the back of his seat. Removing his body required the teams to pull the plane apart. Wiley was wrapped in a sleeping bag and placed next to Rogers on the sandy shore. When all the personal items had been placed in the boats, the bodies were placed on the oomiak and the teams slowly returned to Barrow.

Morgan later recalled the mood of the rescue team, "As we started our slow trip back to Barrow one of the Eskimo boys began to sing a hymn in Eskimo and soon all the voices joined in this singing and continued until our arrival at Barrow when we silently bore the bodies from the beach to the hospital." [6]

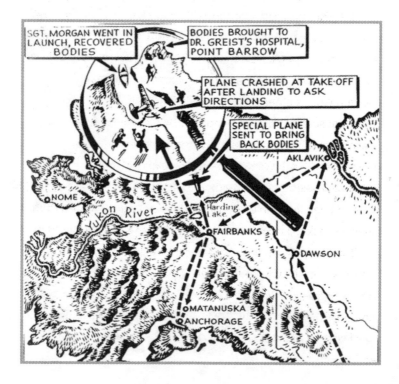

Returning to Barrow, the Eskimos carefully carried the bodies of the two fliers into the hospital. Later, the rescuers would voice their concern to the families of the victims:

We but sorrow with the bereaved families, and would have them know that we did our best for their loved ones, that we worked over their torn bodies as with sacred things...Words are so inadequate, fall so short of being even symbols of ideas, and they fail us. But our hearts are with the suffering. [7]

Sergeant Morgan went back to his radio hut and prepared to share the tragic story with the world. Through radio and telephone, the news of the crash reached the families of the men long before the official telegrams arrived.

Mae Post was visiting friends in Ponca City, Oklahoma, when she received word of Wiley's death. A *New York Times* story reported her response, "Exhausted by grief, Mrs. Post went to bed for several hours." When she recovered, she left for Maysville to be with Wiley's parents and plan his funeral. [8]

Because there was no telephone at the Maysville farm, the town's mayor joined the local newspaper publisher in sharing the sad news with Wiley's parents. Grieving, Mrs. Post said, "This is the news we've been dreading for years." Mr. Post said the family "had been living in dread of this for years and years, but it is such a shock to know that our boy has been killed." [9]

Betty Rogers was with her daughter Mary in Skowhegan, Maine, when she was told of Will's death. Fearful that her son Jimmy had been hurt, she asked, "Has something happened to Jimmy?" [10]

Her sister broke the news, "No Betty, its Will. Will has had an accident."

No one knew northern Alaska better than Joe Crosson, so he and the chief radio man for Pan American took off from Fairbanks in a seaplane with all the passenger seats removed to make room for the bodies of the famous men. On Sunday, 15,000 mourners gathered as the bodies of Wiley and Rogers arrived in Seattle, Washington aboard Crosson's plane.

William Winston took over as pilot for the flights to Los Angeles, where Rogers' body was removed and taken by hearse to the site where his memorial services would be held. Winston then proceeded on to Oklahoma City to deliver Wiley to his home state. Joe Crosson stayed with the body throughout the entire flight. When the aircraft landed in Oklahoma City, 8,000 people stood quietly as Wiley's body was carried from the plane.

The day after the fatal crash, both houses of the United States Congress unanimously authorized the Smithsonian Institution to pay up to $25,000 for the *Winnie Mae* and all of its original equipment. Tributes to Wiley and Rogers came from around the world.

THE END

Flags in Oklahoma were ordered to half-staff. A black crepe bow was tied to the propeller of the *Winnie Mae* in a hangar in Bartlesville. The *Maysville News* dedicated its weekly edition to the tragedy with a large photo of Post and the words, "Wiley Post, the World's Greatest Aviator."

Newspapers throughout the nation devoted front-page headlines and photos to the crash for days. An editorial in *The Daily Oklahoman* described the State's tragic loss:

> *Death is doubly cruel in depriving Oklahoma of her two out-standing citizens...Both of the men who have gone from Oklahoma prairies to win world fame have died in a single day. Only one swing of the scythe of death, and the two best known of all Oklahomans have gone beyond the stars.*
>
> *...The tragedy that darted down from Arctic clouds claimed men who had entrenched themselves in the love and admiration of a world. But this universal sorrow is climaxed in Oklahoma. It is most bitter on the old Cherokee prairies where the people remember Will Rogers as a boy. It is supremely bitter in the fields of broomcorn and among the derricks where Wiley Post first caught the eagle's spirit and resolved to cross clouds and sky...*
>
> *There is nothing Oklahoma can do to add one whit to the fame these men have achieved. One has made his name familiar wherever English words are spoken. The other has set a mark for all future aviators, for no greater birdman has ever defied and conquered skies and seas. Let funeral dirges and the anthems of sorrow attest the grief of Oklahomans, but the achievements of Will Rogers and Wiley Post have built monuments more durable than bronze.* [11]

Newspapers from around the world declared the tragic news of the death of Wiley Post and Will Rogers, in a "crash at the top of the world." *Courtesy of* The Daily Oklahoman.

MOURNING

"It was in flying that Wiley Post found himself…"
—Reverend William Richardson "Billy" White

The funeral procession to Maysville ended in a one-room church where more than 7,000 people stood outside in the summer heat. Nearly two hours went by as family and friends shuffled past Wiley's casket and out the back door of the little church.

President Franklin D. Roosevelt declared Thursday a National Day of Mourning. Will Rogers' funeral was scheduled in California for the same day. *The Daily Oklahoman* lead editorial, entitled "Journey's End," tried to express the grief felt by the state:

It is the melancholy duty of Oklahomans to mourn on a single day the passing of one who has been called the most popular man that ever lived and another one who has been called by competent authorities the greatest flier of all time.. There is but one heart in Oklahoma and that heart is unutterably sore. [1]

As the funeral procession moved on to Oklahoma City, 20,000 people gathered on the south steps of the State Capitol building to pass by Wiley's casket in the capitol rotunda. Less than half of the crowds were able to enter the capitol. At noon, eight national guardsmen carried the casket down the capitol steps. Airplanes flew low overhead, dropping flowers on the crowd below.

Aviation heroes including Amelia Earhart and transatlantic fliers Bennett Griffin and Jimmy Mattern, and record-setting pilot Art Goebel were seated among 2,000 people, while thousands more waited outside. It was the largest funeral in the history of Oklahoma with the crowd estimated to be between 40,000 and 75,000 people.

First Baptist Church's Reverend William Richardson "Billy" White spoke at Wiley's funeral, "He died doing what he wanted to do. Flying was his supreme emotion and passion. It was in flying that Wiley Post found himself. In was in this endeavor that he lived, moved and had his being." [2]

Wiley's body was taken to a mausoleum at Fairlawn Cemetery, where it remained overnight until Mae decided where he would be buried. Though the United States Congress approved his burial at Arlington National Cemetery and Wiley's father wanted his son buried in Maysville, Mae chose Memorial Park Cemetery in far north Oklahoma City, just outside of Edmond.

In Alaska, all 22 United States Signal Corps radio stations observed five minutes of silence at high noon in honor of their fallen hero. *The Daily Oklahoman* paid tribute to Wiley, "…Wiley Post flew solo Thursday night. After the most reverent and highest tribute the nation and state could pay, Wiley Post was as he conquered the world from the air-alone." [3]

AVIATORS REMEMBER

"…I shall always think of Wiley as being the bravest of the brave."
—Amelia Earhart

Newspapers and magazines worldwide carried headline stories of the tragic deaths of Wiley Post and Will Rogers. Many of the greatest tributes came from Wiley's fellow aviators.

American World War I ace, Captain Eddie Rickenbacker, considered Wiley's death "…a serious blow to the science of flying… The pioneering spirit is what set Post apart from the usual run of expert flyers. He saw what ought to be done. Then he found out how to do it. Then he went and did it." [1]

None other than Amelia Earhart called Wiley "the bravest of the brave…In addition to his willingness to share with others anything he had found out about planes or motors, his most dominant characteristic was his complete unconsciousness that what he did had any value or color. So close was he to his profession that he could not see the sheen on his own wings." [2]

Howard Hughes flew around the world in July, 1938 in three days and 19 hours. When asked to compare his flight with Wiley's 1933 flight around the world, he responded, "…Wiley

Post's flight remains the most remarkable flight in history. It can never be duplicated. He did it alone! To make a trip of that kind is beyond comprehension. It's like pulling a rabbit out of a hat or sawing a woman in half." [3]

There is no question that Wiley set aviation records that will never be duplicated. From flying his single-engine airplane around the globe in record breaking time with Gatty as his navigator, to duplicating his flight two years later, cutting 21 hours off his own record while flying solo, Wiley became a national hero and the *Winnie Mae* became an aviation legend. In the decades since Wiley's death, aviators "…still marvel at how the one-eyed pilot from Oklahoma flew around the world alone, in a slow airplane constructed mainly of plywood and wire." [4]

Every advance today in the field of aeronautics stands on the shoulders of a man many refer to as the "…father of modern aviation…Every advance carries a bit of Post's dream." [5]

Amelia Earhart
Courtesy of The Daily Oklahoman.

HONORING WILEY

"Wiley Post was a beacon in the sky for man's dreams of flying toward the stars."
—President Franklin D. Roosevelt

It has been more than seven decades since Wiley Post flew some of the most unique flights in history. Since that time, many memorials have been dedicated in his name.

Mae sold the *Winnie Mae* to the Smithsonian Institution for $25,000 and bought a farm in Ralls, Texas. She never remarried and was buried beside Wiley at Memorial Park Cemetery when she died in 1984.

A new high school in Maysville was built two years after Wiley died and named in his honor, and Wiley Post Elementary School, in northwest Oklahoma City, continues to play a vital role in educating young people in the Putnam City School District.

In 1936, Wiley was awarded posthumously the prestigious gold medal of the Federation Aeronautique Internationale, the highest award given in the field of aviation. At the banquet in his honor, his benefactor, Frank Phillips, said "The luxurious air transports that soar from coast to coast in 14 hours, the clipper ships which fly the ocean, every landing field, every winking beacon, are all in the finest sense a tribute and memorial to Wiley Post."

A bronze plaque was installed at Floyd Bennett Field, commemorating the spot where Wiley landed after his 1933 flight around the world. In addition, the *Winnie Mae* was dismantled and shipped to Washington, D.C. where she was reconstructed and placed on display at the National Air and Space Museum. Wiley's original pressurized flying suit is displayed there as well.

A privately-owned airport near North May and Britton Road in Oklahoma City was named Wiley Post Field soon after the crash. In 1961, Tulakes Airport, Oklahoma City's primary general aviation airport, was renamed Wiley Post Airport. At the airport dedication ceremony, Mae unveiled a bust in the entrance hall of the administration building next to a photograph of Wiley standing by his beloved *Winnie Mae*. She said, "I want to cry but I can't do it here."

On September 26, 1963, the Oklahoma City Chamber of Commerce unveiled Leonard McMurry's life-size statue of Wiley near the Civic Center in downtown Oklahoma City. A statue of another modern pioneer in America's space program, astronaut Thomas P. Stafford, stands in the same park. Honoring Wiley, Stafford once said, "Every time I donned a space suit, I thought of Wiley Post."

The United States government honored Wiley when the Postal Service issued two commemorative airmail stamps in 1979.

On August 16, 1982 the Oklahoma Air National Guard flew a group of Oklahomans to Point Barrow, Alaska for the dedication of a new granite monument across the street from the Wiley

Post-Will Rogers Airport at Barrow. Former Will Rogers Memorial Curator and biographer Dr. Reba Collins, and Will's second son, James, were among the group who attended the ceremony.

Literature also has played a role in memorializing Wiley. In 1999, Bob Burke's biography of Wiley Post, *From Oklahoma to Eternity: The Life of Wiley Post and the Winnie Mae*, won the Oklahoma Book Award for Non-Fiction and become a major incentive for Oklahomans everywhere to celebrate Wiley's life and ensure that he is remembered by future generations.

In November, 2005 the Oklahoma History Center's grand opening included a two ton, three-quarter scale replica of the *Winnie Mae* that continues to dazzle visitors of all ages. The Center also is home to a wealth of unique artifacts from Wiley's life and adventures, including original telegrams sent to Mae following Wiley's death, the instrument panel from the Orion-Explorer that crashed near Point Barrow, Wiley's watch that stopped at 8:18 on August 15, 1935, and a bronze bust of Wiley.

The Wiley Post Memorial Building, once home to the state's historical society, will soon become the home of Oklahoma's highest courts and legal administration.

Today, many posthumous awards, titles, and events honor the contributions Wiley made during his brief, but remarkable, life—the life of a true adventurer, a big dreamer—and the skies will never be the same.

THE PILOT'S CREED

"Oh! I have slipped the surly bonds of Earth..."
—John Gillespie Magee, Jr.

During the difficult days of the Battle of Britain during World War II, while the United States still officially remained neutral, scores of young American men crossed the border into Canada and enlisted with the Royal Canadian Air Force. Though this was an illegal act, enlisting to fight the Nazis had the understood approval of the United States government. One of these courageous men was an 18-year-old named John Gillespie Magee, Jr. He was born in Shanghai, China, in 1922 to an English mother and a Scotch-Irish-American father, both of whom were missionaries.

Following flight training, he was qualified to fly the Supermarine Spitfire. He was soon posted to the newly formed No. 412 Fighter Squadron, RCAF, and sent to England where he flew fighter sweeps over France and England, quickly rising to the rank of Pilot Officer.

On one of his high altitude test flights in 1941, as he soared in the stratosphere in the newest model of the Spitfire V, he was inspired to create a poem. When he returned to base, he wrote a letter to his parents telling them about the verse that "...started at 30,000 feet, and was finished soon after I landed." [1]

On the back of the letter his parents found the poem he had

described to them that he had entitled "High Flight." Just three short months later, and only three days after the United States had officially entered the War, Pilot Officer John Gillespie Magee, Jr. was killed in a mid-air crash as he was descending in the clouds. A farmer later testified that he saw Magee struggling to push back the canopy of his plane. He finally stood up to jump, but he was too close to the ground for his parachute to open and he fell, dying instantly. He was just 19 years old.

Archibald MacLeish, who was then the Librarian of Congress, saw the verse that John had created and included it in an exhibition of poems called "Faith and Freedom," calling Magee "…the first poet of the war." [2] For many years, it was published in various sources, where the layout and punctuation was frequently altered. The original document is in the Manuscript Division of the Library of Congress.

Unexpectedly, the poem that John Magee had written for his parents became a part of most American households in the 1950s through a new invention called television. For many years a film presentation of "High Flight" being read over scenes of mountains, American flags, and fighter aircraft soaring through the clouds was a station closing video on many United States television stations. Because they heard it virtually every evening, people began quoting several beautiful lines of the poem, though they were unaware of the history of the verse. Those captured on Magee's tombstone were the most famous. "Oh! I Have Slipped The Surly Bonds of Earth…Put Out My Hand And Touched the Face of God." [3]

Now that television programming never goes off-line, the poem is no longer a staple in American homes. However, on January 28, 1986, President Ronald Reagan rekindled interest in the famous sonnet when he spoke to the nation the day of the space shuttle explosion. Following his remarks in honor of the lost crew, he concluded with, "…We will never forget them nor the last time we saw them, as they prepared for their mission and waved goodbye and slipped the surly bonds of Earth to touch the face of God." [4]

Over the years, copies and recitations of "High Flight" have been used to honor fallen pilots and war heroes. It is frequently referred to as the "pilot's creed," denoting the beliefs or principles that guide the work of aviators. The complete version of the poem is offered here as a final thought in honor of Wiley's life and remarkable achievements in his beloved field of aviation. It is dedicated to the man who discovered "…the high untrespassed sanctity of space" and whose work paved the way for those brave patrons of flight who followed him into the "…delirious burning blue." [5]

Rudy Post, left, the nephew of Wiley Post, joined filmographer Bill Moore, center, and biographer Bob Burke at the dedication of the Wiley Post Memorial near the gravesites of Wiley and Mae in far north Oklahoma City.

High Flight

Oh! I have slipped the surly bonds of Earth
And danced the skies on laughter-silvered wings;
Sunward I've climbed, and joined the tumbling mirth
Of sun-split clouds, --- and done a hundred things
You have not dreamed of --- wheeled and soared and swung
High in the sunlit silence. Hov'ring there,
I've chased the shouting wind along, and flung
My eager craft through footless halls of air....

Up, up the long, delirious burning blue
I've topped the wind-swept heights with easy grace
Where never lark, nor ever eagle flew ---
And, while with silent, lifting mind I've trod
The high untrespassed sanctity of space,
Put out my hand, and touched the face of God.

--- John Gillespie Magee, Jr. [6]

Mae attends first-day-of-issue ceremonies as two airmail stamps honoring Wiley's life debut in 1969. *Courtesy of Oklahoma Historical Society.*

NOTES

Character in Action:

1. John McCain with Mark Salter, *Character is Destiny: Inspiring Stories Every Young Person Should Know and Every Adult Should Remember.* New York: Random House, 2005.
2. *Ibid.*
3. *Ibid.*

INTRODUCTION – A Pioneer Spirit:

1. *New York Times*, 8-16-35, 8-18-35.
2. Bob Burke, *From Oklahoma to Eternity: The Life of Wiley Post and the Winnie Mae.* Oklahoma City: Oklahoma Heritage Association, 1998.

CHAPTER 1 - The Future Unfolds:

1. Bryan Sterling and Frances Sterling, *Forgotten Eagle.* New York: Carroll & Graf Publishers, 2001.
2. Wiley Post and Harold Gatty, *Around the World in Eight Days.* New York: Garden City Publishing Company, 1931.
3. Sterling, *Forgotten Eagle*, 27.
4. Post, *Eight Days*, 244.
5. Post, *Eight Days*, 245.
6. Post, *Eight Days*, 247.
7. Sterling, *Forgotten Eagle*, 33.

CHAPTER 2 – Falling and Flying:

1. Odie B. Faulk, *Jennys to Jets.* Muskogee, Oklahoma: Western Heritage Books Inc., 1983.
2. Post, *Eight Days*, 251.
3. Parole agreement between Wiley and the Oklahoma Department of Corrections, vertical file of the Oklahoma Historical Society.
4. Post, *Eight Days*, 254-255.
5. Sterling, *Forgotten Eagle*, 49.
6. Post, *Eight Days*, 260.

CHAPTER 3 – The Eye:

1. Sterling, *Forgotten Eagle*, 59.
2. June 16, 1993 interview with Eula Pearl Scott by Bill Pitts, now held by the oral history department of the Oklahoma Historical Society.
3. Sterling, *Forgotten Eagle*, 63
4. Mohler, *Wiley Post*, 7.
5. *Ibid.*

CHAPTER 4 – The Winnie Mae:

1. Post, *Eight Days*, 272
2. Bob Burke, Lyle Boren: *Rebel Congressman.* Oklahoma City, Oklahoma: Oklahoma Heritage Association, 1991, p. 31.
3. Post, *Eight Days*, 277.
4. *Ibid.*, 278.
5. *Ibid.*, 279 - 280.
6. Bryan Sterling and Frances Sterling, *Will Rogers & Wiley Post: Death at Barrow.* New York: M. Evans and Company, Inc., 1993, p. 16.
7. Post, *Eight Days*, 281.

CHAPTER 5 – Get Ready...Get Set

1. Post, *Eight Days*, 22.
2. Post, *Eight Days*, 21.
3. Sterling, *Forgotten Eagle*, 78.
4. Post, *Eight Days*, 60.
5. *Ibid.*, 53.
6. Mohler, *Wiley Post*, 20-21
7. *Ibid.*, 22.
8. *Ibid.*
9. *Ibid.*
10. Post, *Eight Days*, 60.

11. *Ibid.*, 68 - 69.
12. *Ibid.*, 72

CHAPTER 6 – Go!:
1. Post, *Eight Days*, 91-92.
2. *Ibid.*, 92-93.
3. *Ibid.*, 95.
4. *Ibid.*, 103-109.
5. *Ibid.*, 111
6. *Ibid.*, 121.
7. *Ibid.*, 122.
8. *Ibid.*
9. Post, *Eight Days*, 141.
10. *Ibid.*, 151-153.
11. Mohler, *Wiley Post*, 23.
12. Sterling, *Forgotten Eagle*, 98.
13. *Ibid.*, 99.
14. *Ibid.*
15. Post, *Eight Days*, 171 - 172.

CHAPTER 7 – Half Way There:
1. New York Times, 6-28-31.
2. Sterling, *Forgotten Eagle*, 101.
3. Post, *Eight Days*, 183 - 184.
4. *Ibid.*, 187.
5. *Ibid.*, 196.
6. *Ibid.*, 199.
7. *Ibid.*, 200-201.
8. *Ibid.*, 202-203.
9. *Ibid.*, 207-210.

CHAPTER 8 – Eight Days:
1. Post, *Eight Days*, 216.
2. *Ibid.*,
3. *Ibid.*, 217.
4. *Ibid.*, 218.
5. *Ibid.*, 222.
6. *Ibid.*, 223.
7. *Ibid.*, 225.
8. *Ibid.*, 225-226.

9. *Ibid.*, 230.
10. *Ibid.*, 232
11. *New York Times*, 7-2-31.
12. Post, *Eight Days*, 233.
13. *Ibid.*, 234.
14. *Ibid.*, 235.

CHAPTER 9 – Home Again:
1. *New York Times*, 7-3-31.
2. *New York Times*, 7-2-31.
3. Post, *Eight Days*, 235.
4. *New York Times*, 7-4-31.
5. *The Daily Oklahoman*, 7-5-31.
6. *New York Times*, 7-3-31.
7. *Ibid.*
8. *Ibid.*
9. *New York Times*, 6-29-31.
10. Post, *Eight Days*, 11.
11. Mohler, *Wiley Post*, 36.

CHAPTER 10 – Solo:
1. Mohler, *Wiley Post*, 39.
2. *Ibid.*, 46-47.
3. *Ibid.*, 40-41.
4. *New York Times*, 7-16-33.
5. Sterling, *Forgotten Eagle*, 123.
6. *The Daily Oklahoman*, 6-30-33.
7. Mohler, Wiley Post, 51.
8. Sterling, *Forgotten Eagle*, 126.

CHAPTER 11 – Around the World . . . Alone:
1. *New York Times*, 7-16-33.
2. Mohler, *Wiley Post*, 58.
3. *New York Times*, 7-18-33.
4. *Ibid.*, 7-17-33.
5. *Ibid.*, 7-18-33.
6. Mohler, *Wiley Post*, 62.
7. *Ibid.*, 64.
8. *New York Times*, 7-25-33.

9. *Ibid.*, 7-21-33.

10. *Ibid.*, 7-23-33.

11. Mohler, *Wiley Post*, 65.

CHAPTER 12 – New Discoveries and Exciting Inventions:

1. Sterling, *Forgotten Eagle*, 141-142.

2. Mohler, *Wiley Post*, 77.

3. Sterling, *Forgotten Eagle*, 146.

4. *New York Times*, 12-4-34.

5. *Ibid.*

6. Sterling, *Forgotten Eagle*, 152-153.

7. *New York Times*, March, 1935.

8. *New York Times*, 3-6-35.

9. Day, *The Autobiography of Will Rogers*, 383.

CHAPTER 13 – Wiley and Will:

1. Sterling, *Forgotten Eagle*, 166.

2. *Ibid.*, 172-173.

3. *Ibid.*, 170.

4. *Ibid.*, 163.

5. Reba Collins, *Will Rogers and Wiley Post in Alaska.* Claremore, Oklahoma: Will Rogers Heritage Press, 1984.

6. Sterling, *Forgotten Eagle*, 177-178.

7. Collins, *Will Rogers and Wiley Post in Alaska*, 4.

8. *Ibid.*, 8.

9. *Los Angeles Times*, 3-16-36.

10. Sterling, *Forgotten Eagle*, 241-242.

11. Henry W. Greist, *The Northern Cross.* September, 1935.

CHAPTER 14 – The Flight Home:

1. Sterlings' interview with Rose Okpeaha Leavitt, 7-25-86.

2. Greist, *The Northern Cross*, 1.

3. *Akron Times Press*, 8-17-35.

4. *Washington Herald*, 8-17-35.

5. Sterling, *Forgotten Eagle*, 253.

6. Associated Press story of 8-17-35, distributed to the world's newspapers.

7. Greist, *The Northern Cross*, 3.

8. *New York Times*, 8-17-35.

9. *Ibid.*

10. Betty Rogers, *Will Rogers.* 1941.

11. From a survey of newspaper clippings from Collins, Will Rogers.

CHAPTER 15 – A Final Resting Place:

1. *The Daily Oklahoman*, 8-23-35.

2. *Ibid.*

3. *The Daily Oklahoman*, 8-24-35.

CHAPTER 16 – Aviators Remember:

1. *New York Times*, 8-18-35.

2. *Ibid.*

3. Mohler, *Wiley Post*, 12.

4. *Oklahoma Today*, July-August, 1998, 51.

5. *Ibid.*

"Post"script – The Pilot's Creed:

1. www.qunl.com/rees0008.html.

2. *Ibid.*

3. *Ibid.*

4. www.skygod.com/quotes/high-flight.html.

5. *Ibid.*

ERIC DABNEY is a native Oklahoman, born in Oklahoma City and raised in Kremlin. He received his undergraduate and graduate degrees from the University of Central Oklahoma, where he now serves as an adjunct professor, and lives with his wife and three daughters near Guthrie. Eric serves as an associate editor for the Oklahoma Heritage Association and Commonwealth Publishing and is nationally known as a contributing writer for the Historical Publishing Network in San Antonio, Texas. He is the co-author of *Historic South Carolina* and *Willie of the Valley: The Life of Bill Paul.*

JANICE JOHNSON is a native Oklahoman, born in Vinita and raised in Tulsa. She received her B.S. in Elementary Education from Northeastern Oklahoma State University and her M.S. and Ed.D. from Oklahoma State University. She is a retired Professor Emeritus from the University of Central Oklahoma where she taught for almost 30 years. She co-created the graduate degree in Early Childhood Education at UCO and served as curriculum coordinator and graduate student advisor for the program for many years. During her tenure at the University, she taught and supervised scores of teachers-in-training and continued to mentor them as they began their careers and assumed their teaching responsibilities. The mother of two remarkable women, Janice and her husband, Billy, reside in Edmond, Oklahoma.

ABOUT THE ILLUSTRATOR

Sherry Tipton Snyder was born in Texas, reared in Oklahoma, and now lives in Boulder, Colorado. She graduated from Oklahoma City University with a double major in bassoon and piano performance. Self taught, Sherry has done numerous commissioned works, specializing in horses, beloved pets, and people. Her busy life now involves two sons, piano students, earning a black belt in tae-kwon-do, maintaining a household, gardening, and, when time allows, artwork.

INDEX